IEG | **WORLD BANK GROUP**
INDEPENDENT EVALUATION GROUP | World Bank • IFC • MIGA

Knowledge-Based Country Programs

AN EVALUATION OF WORLD BANK GROUP EXPERIENCE

**Library of Congress Cataloging-in-Publication
Data**

Knowledge-based country programs : an
evaluation of World Bank group experience.

    pages cm

  Includes bibliographical references and index.

  ISBN 978-1-4648-0223-2 (alk. paper) — ISBN
978-1-4648-0226-3 (ebook)

  1. World Bank. 2. Economic assistance—
Developing countries. 3. Knowledge
management—Development countries.
HG3881.5.W57K66 2015
  338.9109172'4—dc23

                                    2015005894

Contents

Appendixes

The appendixes to this report are available at

http://ieg.worldbankgroup.org/evaluations/knowledge-based-country-programs

Abbreviations

AAA	analytical and advisory activities	FSAP	Financial Sector Assessment Program
AIDS	acquired immune deficiency syndrome	FY	fiscal year
ART	antiretroviral therapy	GDP	gross domestic product
ASEAN	Association of Southeast Asian Nations	HIV	human immunodeficiency virus
CAS	country assistance strategy	IBRD	International Bank for Reconstruction and Development
CDP	Country Development Partnership	ICA	Investment Climate Assessment
CNDP	complementary national direct payment	IDA	International Development Association
CPAR	Country Procurement Assessment Review	IEG	Independent Evaluation Group
CPIA	Country Policy and Institutional Assessment	IFC	International Finance Corporation
		IMF	International Monetary Fund
CPS	country partnership strategy	IPRCC	International Poverty Reduction Center in China
CPSCR	Country Partnership Strategy Completion Report	JERP	Joint Economic Research Program (Kazakhstan)
CSO	civil society organization	JSP	Joint Studies Program (Chile)
DAC	Development Assistance Committee	KBP	knowledge-based program
DEC	Development Economics Vice Presidency of the World Bank and Chief Economist	KEIAP	Kuwait Education Indicators and Assessment Project
DIPRES	Director of Budgets of the Ministry of Finance (Chile)	LBP	lending-based program
ESW	economic and sector work	M&E	monitoring and evaluation
EU	European Union	MARP	most-at-risk population
FIAS	Foreign Investment Advisory Service	MSME	micro, small, and medium enterprises
FIRST	financial sector reform and strengthening	NCD	non-communicable disease

OECD	Organisation for Economic Co-operation and Development	PSD	private sector development
PBB	performance based budgeting	QAG	Quality Assurance Group
PEFA	public expenditure and financial accountability	RAS	reimbursable advisory services
PEMNA	Public Expenditure Management Network for Asia	RIMSys	Results Integration and Management Systems
PFM	public financial management	ROSC	Report on the Observance of Standards and Codes
PIM	public investment management	SAR	special administrative region
PISA	Program for International Student Assessment	SME	small and medium enterprises
PPP	purchasing power parity	TA	technical assistance
		VCT	voluntary counseling and testing

Acknowledgments

This report of the Independent Evaluation Group (IEG) was prepared by a team led by Aristomene Varoudakis and Juan José Fernández-Ansola that included Mauricio Carrizosa, Victor Macias, and Albert Martinez, with contributions from Richard Burcroff, Susan Ann Caceres, Florence Charlier, Ismail Dalla, William Experton, James Hanson, James Lacey, Hernan Levy, Pia Helene Schneider, Hjalte Sederlof, Xiaolun Sun, Isabelle Tsakok, and Jan Peter Wogart. Analytical support for the review of the World Bank's portfolio of analytic and advisory activities and the evaluation's findings was provided by Aida Tapalova and Erkin Yalcin. William Hurlbut edited the report and Aimée Niane provided administrative support. Following Aristomene Varoudakis's transfer to the Development Economics Vice Presidency in October 2012, Mauricio Carrizosa and Juan José Fernández-Ansola were responsible for revising—in response to management's and other comments—and finalizing the report.

The evaluation benefited from advice and feedback from many persons, in particular the peer reviewers, Shantayanan Devarajan and Shahrokh Fardoust, as well as Martha Ainsworth, Geeta Batra, Hans-Martin Boehmer, Daniela Gressani, Manny Jimenez, Rick Scobey, Mark Sundberg, Marvin Taylor-Dormond, and Christine Wallich. The team gratefully acknowledges the support of management and staff throughout the Bank, and especially in the nine focus countries of the evaluation, who generously shared their time and perspectives with the evaluation team. Special appreciation is extended to many staff and managers, especially in Bank Group country offices, who provided invaluable assistance for the field visits.

The evaluation was conducted under the guidance and supervision of Nick York, Director, Country, Corporate, and Global Evaluations, IEG; and Ali Khadr, Senior Manager, Country, Corporate, and Global Evaluations, IEG, under the general direction of Caroline Heider, Director-General, Evaluation.

Overview | HIGHLIGHTS

This evaluation assesses knowledge-based activities in nine country programs selected from 48 knowledge-intensive programs supported by the Bank Group. It identifies the factors in the success or failure of those activities as they contribute to policy making or development outcomes. It also identifies areas of strength for the Bank Group as well as areas of weakness or risk. The evaluation findings are therefore relevant to current Bank Group efforts to strengthen the contribution of knowledge to development. The evaluation was done on economic and sector work and non-lending technical assistance activities selected from a purposive sample of knowledge-intensive country programs. In addition, the evaluation assessed International Finance Corporation Advisory Services for their synergy with the Bank's analytical and advisory activities. The findings have implications for the Bank Group's knowledge work, including governance and incentives.

The Bank Group remained a strategic partner in the focus countries by providing knowledge services that addressed one or more client needs, which ranged from customized development solutions and capacity development to experience-sharing and innovative ideas. In the sample of countries, the Bank Group was more effective when it worked on specific sectors rather than broad topics, designed tasks to address specific client concerns, customized international best practice to local conditions, generated data to support policy making, and formulated actionable recommendations that fit local administrative and political economy constraints. The Bank Group was less effective when it did not address issues relevant to the client or was unable to follow up consistently with the client on the implementation of advisory activities. Regardless of the level of government that operated as counterpart (central or local), client participation and good monitoring and evaluation systems were key to good results.

The evaluation has implications for Bank Group work and for staff incentives. On Bank Group work, it finds a need to emphasize "how to" options rather than diagnostics and "what to do" recommendations; stay engaged and responsive through implementation phases of advisory activities (using programmatic approaches, for example); use local expertise to enhance the impact of advisory activities; design advisory projects with relevant responses to client concerns; and remain engaged in areas that are relevant to a client country's medium-term development agenda to maintain its capacity to see the big picture and provide multisectoral development solutions. On incentives, an implication is that enhancing the Bank Group's success rate on providing knowledge services will require staff incentives to be in the knowledge services business.

Why Evaluate Knowledge Programs Now?

The World Bank Group is currently engaged in reflection and debate on how to improve the delivery of development support. Part of this debate concerns strengthening the knowledge agenda. The findings of this evaluation are particularly relevant because they speak directly to questions that the institution is deliberating. In particular, they address four key aspects of the "science of delivery": the role of local partners or local knowledge hubs; consultation with clients and other stakeholders in the process of designing knowledge services; delivery of knowledge on issues that are relevant to the client; and improving the way the Bank Group learns from upper-middle-income countries and intermediating this knowledge to other countries.

The main objective of the evaluation is to learn lessons from practices in a focus group of high-income and upper-middle-income countries that have knowledge-based programs with the Bank Group. Over the past 15 years, Bank Group country programs have shifted toward more intensive delivery of knowledge services relative to lending, and this trend is expected to continue. The lessons from this evaluation could help leverage the Bank Group's global knowledge to meet the needs of countries that mainly rely on knowledge services and are not pressed for financing. The nine selected countries are high-income (Kuwait) and upper-middle-income countries with a high share of knowledge services in their programs, a diversified economic structure, no or moderate Bank lending, and fee-based knowledge services.

The 9 countries selected are fairly representative of countries where the World Bank Group is engaged primarily through knowledge services. They are on the top half of a ranking of relative preponderance of knowledge services, with 48 countries fitting a definition of knowledge-based programs. Compared with the average across the 48 knowledge services-intensive programs, the 9 programs selected are fairly typical but have a lower lending to knowledge services ratio; slightly higher share for knowledge services in the country services budget; greater average number of knowledge activities because they include large clients (China and the Russian Federation); slightly higher gross domestic product (GDP) per capita and a significant external current account surplus because they include China and oil producers; a slightly higher Country Policy and Institutional Assessment rating; and about the same average volume of World Bank loans.

The selection was designed to provide useful illustrations of knowledge services effectiveness in the selected countries, not to provide a sample for statistical projection to overall advisory activity assistance to those countries or to the full set of Bank Group clients. Furthermore, the selection of countries that included International Finance Corporation (IFC) Advisory Services was designed to illustrate complementarities and synergies with the Bank in those countries, not to provide a full illustration of IFC Advisory Services effectiveness.

Methodology

The evaluation categorized Bank Group country programs according to the preponderance of knowledge services in program interventions. At one end of the spectrum were lending-based programs with a predominant role for finance and a relatively lower presence of knowledge services. At the other end were knowledge-based programs where knowledge products are at the core of the relationship.

The categorization was then used to purposively select focus countries that make relatively intensive use of the Bank's core knowledge services. The selected countries were Bulgaria, Chile, China, Kazakhstan, Kuwait, Malaysia, the Russian Federation, South Africa, and Thailand. To probe the synergy of the Bank's knowledge services with IFC Advisory Services, the evaluation also examined those services in the focus countries when a government entity was the recipient.

The selection of economic and sector work (ESW), technical assistance (TA), and IFC Advisory Services paid attention to links to the strategic priorities in the country partnership strategy of the focus country. The knowledge services sampling relied on consultations with country management units. The sample includes World Bank knowledge services and IFC Advisory Services delivered over FY05–11. IFC Advisory Services were reviewed in China, Kazakhstan, the Russian Federation, and South Africa. The sample consists of 266 Bank analytical and advisory activities (AAA) and 34 IFC Advisory Services out of a total of 751 Bank AAA products and 185 IFC advisory service projects (to both government and private sector recipients) delivered over FY05-11. Products with similar thematic focus were grouped in clusters of knowledge activities. Thus, the number of activities reviewed was 196 for Bank AAA and 32 for IFC Advisory Services.

The selected knowledge activities in the nine focus countries were assessed against four criteria: relevance of the knowledge activities to the priority needs of the recipients and the key development goals of the client country; technical quality of the activities in leveraging the Bank's global knowledge and conveying relevant and customized expertise to recipients; results achieved; and sustainability of results.

The assessment of outcomes was based on the feedback obtained during country visits and through desk reviews. The assessed progress ranged from tasks that had little or no impact on policies, such as Investment Climate Assessments in Thailand, to tasks with recommendations that were being implemented, but with no visible impact on policies, such as a report on student loans in Chile, and to tasks where development outcomes were already in evidence, such as a report on inequality in China.

Achieving Outcomes: The Main Success Factors

In the focus countries, intended outcomes were fully achieved or likely to be achieved in 47 percent of the knowledge activities reviewed and partly achieved in another 37 percent. The frequency of outcome achievement was broadly equivalent for Bank ESW and TA—the Independent Evaluation Group (IEG) did not find a significant difference in outcomes between the various models of knowledge service delivery. Outcomes of IFC's Advisory Services were achieved in about 38 percent of the small sample of projects reviewed. The achievement of outcomes of knowledge services in the nine focus countries was comparable to that of Bank Group lending operations across regions. The Bank Group was more effective when it worked on specific sectors rather than broad topics; designed tasks to address specific client concerns; customized international best practice to local conditions; generated data to support policy making; and formulated actionable recommendations that fit local administrative and political economy constraints. Regardless of the level of government that operated as counterpart (central or local), client participation and good monitoring and evaluation (M&E) systems were key to good results.

Outcomes were more likely to be achieved when the knowledge services focused on specific sectors, such as agriculture and rural development, education and health, and the financial sector. Reaching outcomes proved more difficult in broader thematic areas, encompassing an ambitious reform agenda, or when the achievement of results required multisector efforts, such as private sector development, economic policy, and public sector governance. In such complex areas, knowledge service results often suffered when new legislation was necessary before the recommended reforms could be implemented. For example, in Kuwait, interactions between parliament and the executive complicated the passing of laws in several areas of Bank TA, such as procurement, public finance, civil service, freedom of information, and anticorruption.

Knowledge services used in the design of lending operations were more likely to succeed than freestanding knowledge services. Although lending was limited in most of the focus countries, it remained a powerful driver of results for the Bank's knowledge services as at least partial achievement of expected outcomes of Bank knowledge services was observed more frequently when knowledge services were used for the design of lending operations. Possible explanations are that in this instance the Bank has more leverage than with freestanding knowledge services, and also that the knowledge services by definition are supporting a program that is expected to be implemented. Freestanding knowledge services many times contributed to policy discussions where the authorities had not yet taken a position.

The achievement of outcomes was not correlated with financing arrangements for knowledge services—Bank or client—probably owing to the high relevance to the client of Bank knowledge services in most of the focus countries. Other factors—related to the relevance of design, quality, timeliness, client participation, and use of local expertise—were more closely associated with achievement of results than source of financing.

Knowledge services requested by the client and designed specifically to achieve client objectives were more likely to achieve outcomes than knowledge services of a more generic character. For example, in China there is evidence that the recommendations of the report *Reducing Inequality for Shared Growth in China: Strategy and Policy Options for Guangdong Province*, a high-profile study conducted jointly with the provincial authorities, are being gradually implemented with concrete results in declining inequality. In Thailand, contrary to other development agencies, counterparts see the Bank as having the capacity to properly customize international best practice to the Thai context because of its knowledge of local institutions that comes mainly from the expertise of staff in the Regional Country Office in Bangkok. The Thai report *The Economics of Effective AIDS Treatment* is a good example of customization to country context. In instances where the Bank did not fully address issues relevant to the client, results of knowledge-based activities tended to be poorer. Knowledge services that lagged in the achievement of outcomes were also weak in conveying international best practice, providing relevant examples, producing new evidence and data useful for policy making, formulating actionable recommendations, and discussing the capacity requirements and administrative feasibility of implementing recommendations.

Knowledge services with fully or partly achieved outcomes were more likely to use local expertise. Use of local experts and counterpart participation appear to help modify global best practices to fit local conditions, formulate recommendations that account for capacity constraints, and improve stakeholder ownership of findings and suggested actions. Client participation in the various stages of knowledge services also was associated with the achievement of results. Moreover, knowledge services that achieved results have more often contributed to strengthening institutions as well as analytical and policy formulation capacity of recipients. The China *Preparation of Capital Market Development* report is an example of detailed coverage of the institutional and policy context and reliance on a local team of experts to draft the report in Chinese using existing data. The report contributed to capacity building at the Research Center of China Securities Regulatory Commission and to raising its profile and role as the capital markets regulator.

The outcomes of about 75 percent of the Bank knowledge services and the IFC Advisory Services were likely to be at least partly sustained. That is, knowledge services were likely to have (at least partial) lasting impacts on policies, capacity, or institutions.

The majority of these knowledge products conveyed international best practice and relevant examples, generated new evidence to inform policy making, and formulated actionable recommendations consistent with the findings. Sustainability of outcomes was more often observed when knowledge services were complemented by other World Bank activities (lending, other ESW, or complementary TA). In the majority of cases where sustainability of outcomes was likely, knowledge services contributed to strengthening institutions or the analytical and policy formulation capacity of recipients. About 60 percent of Bank knowledge services contributed at least partly to developing or strengthening institutions—with a much lower frequency in the case of IFC Advisory Services. Similarly, a large majority of Bank knowledge services and a significant part of IFC Advisory Services contributed to strengthening analytical or policy formulation capacity of recipients.

Areas of Bank Strength

The Bank remained relevant and a strategic partner in the focus countries by providing knowledge services that addressed one or more client needs. Customized development solutions filled a knowledge gap in an area where counterparts needed timely and actionable recommendations to develop a strategy or take action. In experience-sharing and innovative ideas on issues where counterparts had not yet taken a position, the Bank functioned as a sounding board or connected counterparts to cutting-edge international expertise. Capacity development was provided in the form of knowledge that helped build capacity either through training, networking, or access to international best practice. Public knowledge goods typically consisted of Bank-funded reports available to a broad audience primarily for disseminating analyses of developments (such as Economic Monitoring Reports) or particular sectors or issues (such as investment climate assessments and financial sector assessments).

The Bank's main strength, which reflected recommendations from previous IEG knowledge services evaluations, was its ability to fulfill in a timely manner client requests for state-of-the-art advice. Clients found most value in the Bank's ability to address relevant developmental issues, convey international best practice, act as a trusted knowledge broker, customize knowledge to the local context, and take a pragmatic approach to important issues that required multisectoral development solutions. Counterparts interviewed by IEG acknowledged four key strengths: ability to benchmark against international best practice through cross-country comparisons, reputation as an independent and credible broker of knowledge with a partnership approach, knowledge of the local context and capacity to customize international best practice solutions, and capacity to see the big picture and analyze cross-sectoral issues important for development. Timely delivery of knowledge services to affect important decisions was essential to achieve the expected outcomes.

Another key strength was linked to its role as "knowledge connector." The Bank's convening power was often used to mobilize top international experts for brainstorming sessions and seminars with high-level government officials, or for TA and working sessions with government agencies. There are some good examples where the Bank's knowledge activities facilitated South-South exchanges and policy dialogue in the focus countries. The Bank has used mostly its informal networks, through the task team leaders and network management, to convey knowledge acquired in Chile to other countries in the Latin American region and elsewhere. In Kazakhstan, some government agencies have already shared their experiences with other countries in the region. But more can be done as the Bank's geographic, thematic, and organizational fragmentation prevents the full potential of such exchanges from being realized. In China, for example, while the World Bank Institute's technical assistance work has focused on catalyzing lessons for other development countries, it appears that the Bank has not fully exploited the potential of this mutual lending opportunity. The Russian Federation could benefit from the extensive work the Bank has done in China on regional approaches to investment promotion, but lessons from this experience have not been transmitted to the Russian Federation.

Bank knowledge services and IFC Advisory Services generally complemented one another in contributing to results, despite some gaps. In a few cases there were well-defined programs of joint World Bank and IFC knowledge activities. For example in South Africa, to ensure synergy and coordination, IFC used experienced Bank staff to manage projects on enterprise tax burden and compliance. Other examples are in the investment climate area, where World Bank–IFC collaboration allowed both to contribute to policy dialogue and reform activities. But overall the experience with coordination between World Bank and IFC was mixed. Coordination can be improved, for example, by establishing more systematic mechanisms for inclusion of one institution in the other's review processes, especially at the concept and design stage. A key factor supporting the synergy of the two institutions in achieving results was the quality of the results framework in the country partnership strategy (CPS). The articulation of strategic outcomes and the clarity of links between the Bank Group's programs, projects, and instruments with expected outcomes reinforced good joint work. Another factor was the existence of core ESW—such as investment climate assessments and financial sector assessments—which underpinned the strategy and helped identify priorities for improving the investment climate and developing the financial sector.

Areas of Bank Weakness or Risk

Poor achievement of outcomes was associated with weaknesses in relevance of design, quality, timeliness of delivery, or client participation, and little use of local expertise. Knowledge services that lagged in the achievement of outcomes were also weak in conveying international best practice, providing relevant examples, producing new evidence and data useful for policy making, formulating actionable recommendations, and discussing the capacity requirements and administrative feasibility of implementing recommendations. Where the Bank was less able to address issues relevant to the client it also tended to achieve poorer results. The lack of timely delivery of knowledge services to affect important decisions—not a prevalent problem in the sample of countries—also was associated with poorer outcomes.

The Bank's ability to customize knowledge services to the local context and to deliver multisectoral solutions is at risk of eroding where country knowledge is too shallow or too narrow. This risk arises mainly when the Bank works through Reimbursable Advisory Services (RAS) and does not maintain a local presence. The Bank's strengths may also be challenged by its increasing tendency to deliver knowledge services through the "consultant firm model," with insufficient follow up and emphasis on important issues for the medium-term development agenda. There is a tension between the Bank as a development agency—focusing on important medium-term development issues—and the Bank providing specific solutions to narrower problems suggested by the main counterpart in the country—generally a unit within the Ministry of Finance. To the extent that such a unit mars the Bank's engagement in relevant broader development issues, the Bank's overall mission in the country could be impaired. This tension on who is the client needs to be resolved case-by-case using substantial diplomatic tact but emphasizing the Bank's broader development mandate.

Monitoring of Bank knowledge services results was weak—both for individual activities and for country programs. In only 17 percent of the knowledge activities assessed was there at least a partial results framework in the CPS, allowing a tracking of the contribution of the activity to the broader development outcomes sought by the CPS. Similarly, only 23 percent of the knowledge services included, at least partly, result indicators to track the achievement of the activity's outcomes. In contrast to Bank knowledge services, the great majority of IFC Advisory Services reviewed by IEG were at least partly equipped with results indicators to trace achievement of outcomes. Monitoring of capacity development outcomes and lesson learning were, on average, weak for Bank knowledge services, but less so in the case of knowledge services with outcomes likely to be achieved.

Implications for Bank Group Work

▶ Emphasize the "how to" options, as opposed to the diagnostics and the "what to do" recommendations, to enhance client ability to own final policy decisions, action plans, or strategies. In general, tasks that achieved results provided actionable recommendations more often than those that did not achieve results. IEG recommends the Bank give staff more time to interact with clients and local partners and knowledge hubs, including through adequate field presence. Moreover, use analytical resources intensively to ensure that high-quality research underpins recommendations, and deploy high-level consultant expertise able to provide practical know-how and enable customization of global practice.

▶ Stay engaged and responsive in the implementation phases of advisory activities through instruments that help clients translate recommendations from sound analysis into actions that fit local political and administrative constraints. Use of programmatic approaches was important to achieve outcomes. IEG recommends the Bank design programmatic knowledge services in a number of well-defined thematic areas (such as public financial management) that build on initial work to support implementation phases, including engagement of a broad range of stakeholders to help disseminate the reform agenda and maintain the focus on key policy issues in the public domain.

▶ Where applicable, ensure links among Bank ESW, non-lending TA, and projects to help sustain results. When knowledge services were complemented with lending, results were more likely to be sustained. IEG recommends the Bank design CPSs with closer links between knowledge services and lending, including programmatic series deploying both instruments to support the paths from consideration of policy options to implementation of the approaches selected.

▶ Clarify the political economy of reform and use local expertise to enhance the impact of knowledge services. Local partners and Bank Group hubs can be critical in conveying relevant country context considerations. Most of the tasks reviewed referred to the local policy context in varying levels of detail. Those that achieved results probed more deeply into the country context and used local expertise more often than those that did not achieve results. IEG recommends the Bank involve local experts, partners, and local knowledge hubs more extensively in knowledge services to help better understand the political economy of reform in the country where advice is sought, bridge the gap between international good practices and local conditions, enhance the applicability of the recommendations, and build the local capacity to achieve longer-term impact.

▶ Pay attention to the quality and relevance of knowledge services. This is essential for obtaining results—regardless of the form of financing of knowledge services—and for shaping learning under the Bank's "science of delivery." Staff needs to take multiple actions to achieve results: design projects with relevant responses to client concerns; customize international best practice to local conditions, including capacity constraints; generate data to support evidence-based policy making; formulate actionable recommendations that fit local administrative and political economy constraints; and deliver products in time to influence key decisions. IEG recommends the Bank consult broadly with the client and other stakeholders on the issues to be addressed, deploy highly experienced staff with global perspective and ability to deliver knowledge services on time, and adhere to the mandatory knowledge services quality assurance process. The Bank Group should encourage emerging "knowledge hubs" to follow approaches along these lines.

▶ Strengthen synergies between World Bank knowledge services and IFC Advisory Services projects to improve results. Linking Bank and IFC activities also helped achieve results. But experience with Bank–IFC coordination has been mixed, with quality of the CPS results framework and the existence of core ESW among the factors that influenced the degree to which World Bank and IFC knowledge services had synergy. IEG recommends the Bank conduct core knowledge services for private and financial sector development and develop joint Bank–IFC programs and projects within the CPS results frameworks that articulate the outcomes and their linkages with the programs and instruments of both institutions. Complement this with formal mechanisms of including each institution in the other's review processes and better coordination in the field.

▶ Remain engaged in areas that are relevant to a client country's medium-term development agenda to maintain the capacity to see the big picture and provide multisectoral development solutions. This capacity has been a strong point, generally valued by clients, of the Bank's knowledge services. Delivery of knowledge services through a "consultant firm model," which reflects a drive to accommodate multiple and unforeseen needs, often results in fragmentation of Reimbursable Advisory Services (RAS) programs—for example, by dropping tasks linked to medium-term objectives to accommodate shorter-term needs—and may dilute the focus on important medium-term development issues. For countries where most of the activities are knowledge-based and the Bank Group does not have a CPS, IEG recommends that the Bank Group prepare CPSs (which do not have to follow a burdensome consultation process) to provide guidance on engagement objectives and avoid fragmentation of knowledge services away from evolving development priorities. Furthermore, the Bank may consider using instruments (such as high-level brainstorming, conferences, and ESW, including periodic Economic Monitoring Reports) and committing the necessary resources to identify, follow up, and sustain emphasis on issues that are important for medium-term development.

▶ Undertake broad-based consultations and dissemination, acknowledging the public good function of Bank knowledge services while paying attention to local circumstances. Client participation in the different stages of knowledge services appears to be closely associated with success in achieving expected knowledge service outcomes. IEG recommends the Bank broaden the participation of various stakeholders into knowledge-based country programs (for example, by opening up discussions or focus groups with local experts and civil society organizations) and make Bank studies more widely accessible (for example, by recognizing the public good component in knowledge products and sharing a portion of the knowledge services cost with the client on the condition of its disclosure).

▶ Monitor closely implementation and results to track progress toward mutually agreed outcomes and mitigate the risk of fragmentation and loss of strategic focus that are intrinsic to RAS. Bank knowledge services were not monitored and evaluated consistently in the sample of countries. Where M&E was better, knowledge services results were more likely to be achieved, probably reflecting a link between M&E, knowledge service quality, and impact. IEG recommends the Bank use—and continuously improve—implementation and results monitoring systems that would track progress toward achieving the outcomes in the results framework of the CPS and that knowledge activities be more tightly linked with CPS milestones and outcome indicators. A "circle of continuous quality improvement" for M&E is critical for shaping the "science of delivery" that the Bank is presently intent upon and to help improve M&E at the country level.

▶ Reinforce knowledge services governance and partnerships to help enhance results. Governance will benefit from management leadership to encourage knowledge services and develop stronger M&E for knowledge services. World Bank–IFC coordination can be strengthened by developing high-quality CPS results frameworks that clearly articulate links between outcomes and World Bank Group advisory activities, and by establishing more systematic mechanisms to include each organization in the other's review processes. An additional challenge—given the vision of a Bank Group for the whole world—will be to bring in the knowledge acquired from knowledge-based partnerships to lower-income countries.

▶ Strengthen Bank learning from upper-middle-income countries and the intermediation of this knowledge to other countries. There were ample opportunities for learning from development experiences in the focus countries (for example, on the development trajectory from a low-income to an upper-middle-income economy in Malaysia or the extensive work the Bank has done in China on regional approaches to investment promotion). IEG recommends the Bank enhance exchanges of knowledge within the Bank through communities of practice and outside the Bank through networks of practitioners or knowledge hubs; enhance the links of the Bank's regional chief economists with regional institutions that can play a role in sharing the Bank's analytical work; ease the confidentiality of knowledge activities conducted through RAS; and leverage the technical capacity developed by upper-middle-income clients to other countries (for example, partner with Thai institutions to bring in the experience of Thailand's built capacity in banking, payments system, and financial markets to other countries that may need it).

▶ Continue to use RAS to expand the feasible set of Bank services, ensure the sustainability of the Bank's business model in knowledge-based country programs, and generate new knowledge that the Bank can then intermediate to lower-income countries. Although the relevance of RAS is strengthened by client demand and financial commitment, results do not appear significantly different from those of knowledge services funded by the Bank's own resources. Other fundamental success factors—related to the relevance of design, quality, timeliness, client participation, use of local expertise—are more closely associated with the achievement of results. IEG recommends the Bank move decisively toward RAS in knowledge-based programs to sustain this business line, while clarifying the types of knowledge services that come close to "public knowledge goods" (Bank-funded reports targeted to a broad audience to disseminate analyses of developments or particular sectors or issues), as opposed to those that serve specific needs of counterparts. RAS could be offered to institutions that can cover the full cost of the Bank's services, with cost-sharing of knowledge activities that are not pure public knowledge goods. The cost-sharing would recognize the relevance of the activities for other countries and provide for their wider disclosure or dissemination by the recipient or for equalization of access to the Bank's knowledge services among subnational clients with varying capacity to pay for the service. For countries involved in cost-sharing—Chile and Kazakhstan, for example—the disclosure or dissemination to other clients would give them a sense of contributing to the global public knowledge goods agenda. Where there is full cost recovery, it could include the cost of a client survey with the aim of informing both the Bank and the client about the relevance, quality, use, and results achieved or likely to be achieved.

Implications for Staff Incentives

▶ Enhancing the Bank Group's success rate on providing knowledge services will require that the highest-caliber staff have incentives to be in the knowledge services business. There is a perception among Bank staff that lending experience is essential for promotion. At the same time, the world recognizes that knowledge is the foundation of development, and that the Bank should do more in this regard. The incentives for staff to engage in knowledge activities need to be as strong as those for being part of lending operations. At a minimum the Bank should review the incentive system for staff, ensure that knowledge contributions are recognized for career advancement; make bringing knowledge to countries a visible priority; and ensure that personal reputations of staff are enhanced by knowledge contributions. This evaluation suggests the need to deploy part of the best staff in the institution to knowledge services. Those dimensions that got in the way of achieving results in some instances—poor design relevance; weaknesses in conveying international best practice, providing relevant examples, producing new evidence and data useful for policy making, formulating actionable recommendations, or discussing the capacity requirements and administrative feasibility of implementing recommendations—should be addressed by allocating high-caliber staff to the provision of knowledge services. Such staff would also be able to address issues relevant to the client—one of the key factors in achieving successful knowledge service outcomes. Staff incentives for knowledge activities will need to be balanced with rewards for engaging in other important priorities such as lending and work in fragile states.

Management Response | EXECUTIVE SUMMARY

World Bank Group management thanks the Independent Evaluation Group (IEG) for undertaking this valuable evaluation of knowledge-based programs in eight upper-middle-income countries and one high-income country. Management welcomes the opportunity to comment on the draft evaluation report. This is timely in view of the Bank Group's increased focus on measuring results in its knowledge activities.

The next section summarizes World Bank Group response to the evaluation. Management's specific response to IEG's recommendations, with which it generally agrees, is noted in the attached draft Management Action Record (MAR) matrix.

World Bank Management Response

This is a well-written report with useful lessons as the Bank moves forward on the knowledge agenda at the country and global levels. The analysis tackles some important issues ranging from staff incentives to internal and external factors of success and the report skillfully captures and synthesizes the key messages. Management welcomes the thrust of many of the overall findings, which, in general, endorse much of the Bank's approach to knowledge-based work.

The fact that our knowledge services (in these "knowledge-based country programs") are judged to be relevant and generally well regarded by our clients is encouraging. In particular, the report notes that 84 percent of the Knowledge and Advisory Services (with a focus on the Bank's Economic and Sector Work/Technical Assistance or ESW/TA) had fully achieved or partially achieved objectives. Likewise, it is encouraging that "state-of-the-art advice" and "knowledge connector" are seen as Bank strengths. Appendix G of the paper also notes that for countries such as Chile and Bulgaria, the Bank compares favorably to other international institutions, think tanks, and global consulting firms regarding quality, relevance, and timeliness of its knowledge. All of this points to a significant vote of client confidence in the Bank.

Management is in broad agreement with the recommendations made in the report (and summarized in the attached matrix). Implementation of many of the recommendations are already underway. However, we also note that the scope of the evaluation does not fully represent the full range of the Bank's knowledge services; it limits the definition of knowledge-based programs largely to upper-middle-income countries (UMICs) and excludes the vast knowledge base that underpins programs in International Development Association (IDA) and fragile countries; and it does not reflect actions taken to strengthen the results framework, adopted in FY11 and that are summarized in Box 1.

It is important to note that the study does not fully represent the full scope of the Bank's knowledge work in client countries. The work does not acknowledge the fact that all of the Bank's country programs are knowledge-based or have a strong knowledge content. What distinguishes the set of activities covered by this evaluation is not so much the presence of knowledge as the absence of lending. In some of our country programs which do include borrowing, the amount of knowledge work is much greater than in some of the countries covered by this study. We would suggest IEG consider modifying the title of this evaluation as it currently seems to imply it covered all of the Bank's knowledge work, when it is actually limited to nine country programs in middle- and high-income countries.

It is also important to note that the report focuses mainly on ESW/TA, which comprises about 60 percent of the Bank's core knowledge services. While ESW/TA is a critical element of the

> **BOX 1** Progress in Developing a Results Framework for Knowledge since FY11
>
> - The following actions have been taken to strengthen results since the IEG evaluation:
>
> - ESW/TA intermediate outcome indicators have been updated to be more outcome-oriented.
>
> - The task team self-assessment process has been strengthened and hardwired into the Bank's management information system.
>
> - Tools for managers to facilitate greater oversight of quality are now captured in the Ops Portal.
>
> - Guidelines have been developed for reimbursable advisory services (RAS) that facilitates consistency in processing steps and quality assurance across the Bank.
>
> - Client feedback instruments have been put in place for ESW/TA/TE and KP that has been used with the self-assessment to analyze results.
>
> - Programmatic ESW/TA has been adopted to strengthen the strategic orientation of the Bank's knowledge work. This approach is being expanded to accommodate other knowledge products.

Bank's work, management would appreciate an understanding of whether and how IEG proposes to evaluate the remaining core knowledge services, which represent nearly $300 million in expenditures each year.

The report also notes key areas for improvement related to: relevance and technical quality; strategic orientation and sustained follow-up of its knowledge work (particularly in cases where RAS is the primary form of engagement); results focus through strengthening the monitoring and evaluation framework for knowledge; and incentives for knowledge work. The rest of this section outlines the main recommendations and the Bank's response.

The report recommends that the Bank ensure relevance and technical quality through the customization of international evidence to formulate policy options that fit local conditions and generate data to support policy making. This is also linked to the recommendation that the World Bank Group clarify the political economy of reform and use local expertise to enhance the impact of knowledge work. It notes that those knowledge activities that achieved results probed more deeply into the country context and used local expertise more often than those that did not achieve results. The use of local experts, partners, and local think tanks help to better understand the political economy of reform in the country where advice is sought, bridge the gap between international good practices and local conditions, enhance the relevance and applicability of the recommendations, and build the local capacity to achieve longer-term impact.

The report recommends that the Bank Group be more strategic, including putting in place mechanisms for follow-up and sustained engagement. This requires that the Bank stay engaged and responsive in the implementation phases of advisory activities through appropriate instruments that help clients translate recommendations from sound analysis into actions that fit local political and administrative constraints. The report makes the link between the use of programmatic approaches as a tool for sustained engagement and the achievement of high-impact or greater results. The Bank has developed and operationalized a framework (including an approach to monitoring and evaluation) and the allocation of resources that enables use of an explicit programmatic approach (PA). This tool became available on the Operations Portal in FY13.

▶ Reimbursable Advisory Services. The report also notes the need to manage RASs more strategically. A new tool for managing RAS became available on the Operations Portal in FY13. Discussions with Bank management and the Board about the RAS strategy are ongoing.

A FY12 review of RAS (at the time called Fee-Based Services or Reimbursable Technical Assistance) was completed in October of 2012 ("RAS Review"). The review showed that the nature and amounts of RAS are growing and rapidly evolving. Given the importance of

RAS for UMICs, management particularly welcomes the report's assessment of this aspect of the Bank's knowledge work. IEG findings raised issues around confidentiality which may be hampering the extent of broad-based engagement and dissemination of the Bank's knowledge work in client countries. The report also highlighted the tensions around the "consultancy firm" model that is potentially limiting the Bank's ability to engage strategically and emphasize broader development issues in a given country. Despite these challenges, IEG recommends the Bank move decisively towards RAS in knowledge-based programs to sustain this business line. Recommendations also highlighted the need to have the right incentives in place for RAS knowledge work to maintain a focus on development outcomes.

The Bank has been grappling with the above issues (most of which were also addressed in the 2011 RAS review). Management has the following comments related to confidentiality, quality assurance, and the "consultancy firm" model and associated risks.

▶ On confidentiality. The report proposes that the Bank seek to relax some of the confidentiality surrounding RAS. The RAS Review (2012) did look at this issue and the confidentiality guidance for RAS engagements was consequently amended to allow for more openness, with policy guidance to seek client consent for disclosure on a regular basis. The changes were constrained by the Access to Information Policy (AIP), which treats RAS differently from other Bank operations, requiring client consent for disclosure.

▶ On quality assurance. The RAS Review also looked at quality assurance issues and identified this as a priority area for improving the program. Quality assurance for RAS is, in theory, analogous to that of Bank knowledge operations. The modalities for putting this in practice have now been fully elaborated and adopted. The new three pronged approach to monitoring results is also being applied to RAS. Operational Policy and Country Services (OPCS) (with others) has undertaken a number of steps to ensure this approach is tailored to the peculiarities of RAS, including through integrating RAS into the Operations Portal — i.e., the Bank's management information system for knowledge — and through detailed guidance on the application of operational policies to the RAS program.

The report raises a number of issues around the *'consultancy firm'* model. In this connection, management would like to point out that, as an institution, the Bank has never taken the policy position that it can or should act as a consultancy firm. This position underlies a number of the features of the RAS program, including the provision that the Bank does not engage in competitive processes for RAS work. Similarly, it informs a number of the provisions in the model RAS legal agreement on intellectual property and liability, among other things. The issue was considered both in 2008 and during the FY12 RAS Review of the program, since the Bank is often under pressure from clients to conform more closely to private sector practices. On both occasions, the consensus was that the Bank should not follow a private sector business model, as it would be inconsistent with the Bank's mandate and status as an international financial institution. Having noted this, management recognizes the tensions and incentives in a budget constrained environment toward the "consultancy firm" model. Recently adopted policies and guidance on when to undertake a RAS and the related rules and standards around quality assurance, legal agreements, and risks are designed to manage these tensions and related risks.

The report recommends that the Bank Group improve the results measurement system for knowledge services. The weakness in monitoring ESW/TA over the period of the review (FY2005–11) is rightly noted in the report. Since FY11, the Bank has adopted a new three-pronged approach to results and measurement for knowledge (that applies to all client-facing knowledge including RAS). The approach involves: (i) strengthening the self-assessments; and this will build on recommendations from IEG's ongoing review of ESW/TA in the Operations Portal; (ii) implementing client feedback instruments to elicit client assessment of the usefulness and relevance of our knowledge products; and (iii) ex-post review of Bank assessments by IEG (or other external evaluators). This approach is now under implementation for all external client-facing products and for internal knowledge products.

Work is ongoing through systems improvement to reflect both stronger results monitoring and streamlined accountability across all products (lending and knowledge services). In addition, the framework encourages staff to think in terms of a theory of change with clear monitoring indicators to help task teams structure their knowledge activities. This could be applied to specific knowledge products (including ESW/TA) that are linked to the CPS results frameworks. The framework also requires teams to assess the risks associated with the knowledge activity achieving its intended objective, including an assessment of the relevant stakeholders and change agents and actions to mitigate these risks. The aim is to have the resulting plans for risk mitigation, supported by stakeholder analysis. These would reinforce the need to engage local actors to better manage risks associated with the political economy of the knowledge activity or engagement.

The report highlights the need to strengthen incentives for knowledge work ensuring that the appropriate resources and staff are deployed. The report recommends adoption of a financial and budget framework that balances managerial incentives for lending and knowledge activities. The Bank has already initiated actions to improve management oversight to signal senior management's increased attention to results-oriented knowledge work. In addition to the actions outlined in the paragraphs above, the Bank has adopted an approach to link client feedback to management through the memoranda of understanding (MoUs) of regional and network vice presidents. These actions coupled with the broader focus on results and client orientation will help support the appropriate incentives for knowledge work.

IEG's Recommendations

Management agrees with the key recommendations on ways to strengthen quality, client, and results orientation, including incentives for knowledge work. Specifically, the report states the Bank should focus on "how to" options rather than diagnostics and "what to do" recommendations; stay engaged and responsive through implementation phases of advisory activities (including through programmatic approaches); use local expertise to enhance the impact of advisory activities; design advisory projects with relevant responses to client concerns; and ensure the Bank's engagement is strategic with a focus on contributions to outcomes that are relevant to a client country's medium-term development agenda.

Since the period under review in the report, management has initiated a number of actions to strengthen accountability and results orientation. Specifically, management notes that it has already been actively implementing many activities recommended by IEG, as noted in the attached MAR matrix. The allocation of resources to support knowledge products is already driven by the country program's expected results via the country assistance strategy (CAS)/ CPS for result processes. Client and Bank teams determine the development outcomes and the Bank's activities needed to support the outcomes. Resources are then allocated to support the required activities. In many cases these are stand-alone knowledge products that are unrelated to lending. While management is committed to align incentives to achieve excellence in knowledge services, and, in general, to achieve improved development results, it cannot commit to specific budget allocation principles at the time when the entire budget process is being reviewed to align it to the new World Bank Group strategy under development.

Management sees IEG playing a key role in strengthening the monitoring and ex-post evaluation of the Bank Group's knowledge services. Specifically, management looks forward to receiving the results of IEG's ongoing review of the Bank's information management system for knowledge to ensure it will adequately support decision making and ex-post evaluation. Results of the review will be used to further strengthen existing systems and processes for capturing and assessing knowledge.

International Finance Corporation Management Response

International Finance Corporation (IFC) management welcomes IEG's recognition of the many reforms IFC has introduced in recent years to strengthen the impact and effectiveness of our Advisory Services projects. Since most of the limited number of IFC projects reviewed in this report were designed prior to those reforms, care should be taken in interpreting them as representative of IFC's current approach.

Management Action Record

Ensuring Relevance and Technical Quality

IEG FINDINGS & CONCLUSIONS

Relevance and technical quality of results were key drivers for achievement of results of knowledge services. Key dimensions included designing tasks that responded to client concerns; customizing international best practice to local conditions; generating data to support policy making; and delivering products in a timely way to influence key decisions. Moreover, client participation in the different stages of knowledge activities appears to be closely associated with success in achieving expected knowledge service outcomes, and tasks that achieved results provided actionable recommendations more often than those that did not achieve results.

IEG RECOMMENDATIONS

Ensuring relevance and technical quality: Customize international evidence to formulate policy options that fit local conditions and generate data to support policy making. Deploy highly experienced staff with global perspective, and strengthen quality assurance process for knowledge services.

ACCEPTANCE BY MANAGEMENT OF RECOMMENDATION

WB: Agree

MANAGEMENT RESPONSE

WB: We agree with the need to ensure relevance and technical quality. As noted in the findings, we see the most effective way to do this is to work closely with the client to develop actionable recommendations that address the key development objectives/goals. Implementation of this recommendation is already underway.

Various evaluations at the Bank show that the Bank's knowledge is rated well in terms of technical quality (i.e., IEG's 2008 evaluation of ESW/TA; the most recent client surveys both the product based Client Feedback Instrument or CFI, and the Country Opinion Survey Program or COSP). These same instruments highlight the need for stronger client engagement. The Bank is strengthening the monitoring and reporting system that tracks partnerships and client engagement for knowledge.

Quality assurance continues to be strengthened and a number of changes have been implemented since this report was completed: the results framework for ESW/TA was strengthened to be more outcome-oriented; the self-assessment process was strengthened and hardwired into the Bank's management information system with tools managers can use for greater oversight of quality; more systematic guidelines for RAS that facilitates consistency in processing steps and quality assurance across the Bank are in place; finally, the Bank's improved system for quality assurance makes provision for capturing lessons learned in searchable fields that will enable greater learning and data to support policy advice.

Making Use of Political Economy Analysis and Local Knowledge

IEG FINDINGS & CONCLUSIONS

Most tasks referred to the local policy context. Those that achieved results probed more deeply into the local context, used local expertise more often than those that did not achieve results, and formulated actionable recommendations to fit local administrative and political economy constraints. Understanding the political economy of reform and using local expertise can enhance the impact of the Bank's knowledge services. Local partners or hubs can also play a critical role in conveying relevant country context considerations.

IEG RECOMMENDATIONS

Making use of political economy analysis and local knowledge: Involve local experts, partners and local think tanks extensively in knowledge services to help understand better the political economy of reform, bridge the gap between international good practices and local conditions, enhance the applicability of the recommendations, and build local capacity to achieve longer-term impact. Stay engaged with client, know the local context, and strengthen implementation by mobilizing international expertise in a timely fashion. Involve local partners in monitoring and evaluation. When appropriate, engage a broad range of stakeholders to help support the reform agenda and maintain the focus on key policy issues in the public domain. Encourage emerging knowledge hubs to follow approaches along these lines.

ACCEPTANCE BY MANAGEMENT OF RECOMMENDATION

WB: Agree

MANAGEMENT RESPONSE

WB: Implementation of this recommendation is already underway. We agree that consideration of political economy issues are critical and we have initiated consultation around how to strengthen this aspect of our work. Already, as part of the recent improvements to strengthen client and results orientation, we are requiring task teams to explicitly outline the risks they see to the achievement of targeted objectives for a knowledge activity, and client adoption of recommendations. Teams will be asked to identify risks related to design of the knowledge activity/engagement, in line with the approach used for lending services, and within the strategic context of the Bank's country engagement through the CAS/CPS. Guidance and learning material to support staff are being developed. Going forward, a question will be included in the CFI to help monitor the use of local institutions and civil society.

The Bank will also strengthen its approach to improved learning from operations (based on case studies and toolkits). Steps will also be taken to promote shorter learning loops by linking IEG lessons to the project management portal. This will better support teams to analyze the context of specific

Bank engagements to be able to adapt and adjust in a more flexible and timely manner. Recently, a mandatory task team leader (TTL) accreditation program has been launched using experiential and case-based learning as well as on-the-job learning to strengthen staff capacity in results-focused project design, implementation, and client engagement.

Strengthening Engagement and Results Through Multi-Year Frameworks

IEG FINDINGS & CONCLUSIONS

The use of programmatic approaches was important to achieve outcomes, as shown by examples of knowledge services that enabled technical assistance or economic sector work to follow up on initial work. By contrast, some projects launched in response to demand from certain agencies did not produce strong results, sometimes because these were one-off initiatives with poor sustainability prospects. Staying engaged and responsive in the implementation phases of advisory services through appropriate instruments can help clients translate recommendations from sound analysis into actions that fit local political and administrative constraints. By the same token, the focus on reimbursable advisory services to respond to client demand may entail a lack of continuous engagement in some areas or lack of coverage of thematic areas that may not rank sufficiently high on the short-term priorities of clients. The Bank's capacity to see the big picture and provide multi-sector development solutions—strength of the Bank's knowledge services valued by clients—may thus be eroded.

IEG RECOMMENDATIONS

Strengthening engagement and results through multi-year frameworks: Design programmatic knowledge services where appropriate in a number of thematic areas. Ensure that up to date knowledge and/or high-quality research underpins recommendations and provide practical know-how and customization of global practice. Develop and apply principles to ensure balance between strategic (non-reimbursable) and reimbursable activities.

ACCEPTANCE BY MANAGEMENT OF RECOMMENDATION

WB: Agree

MANAGEMENT RESPONSE

WB: The Bank's knowledge work (both RAS and non-RAS) are programmed in a strategic medium-term framework defined by the CPS or CAS. CPSs/CASs are now designed to be results-based and include both lending and knowledge services. Furthermore, quality assurance processes, results measurement, and monitoring have been strengthened for both RAS and non-RAS activities, including for just-in-time advice which is increasingly demanded by our clients. It is therefore incorrect to imply that only non-RAS activities are strategic or that RAS activities are not strategic.

The recommendation to develop and apply principles to ensure balance between RAS and non-RAS activities has already been implemented. Recently adopted quality assurance processes and systems have been used to strengthen the link between individual knowledge activities and the CPS/CAS results. First, teams are now required to clearly outline the objectives and intended audience, along with the intermediate outcomes that will be used to measure progress toward objectives. These objectives and outcomes are required to contribute to one of the overarching outcomes of CPSs/CASs, for those countries that have a CPS/CAS. For those countries that do not have a CPS/CAS (usually high-income countries), teams will still be required to clearly indicate the objective and audience, intended contribution to development outcomes, and related indicators of success. Second, these changes now apply also to RAS and new templates/tools have been designed for teams to ensure that the quality and strategic orientation of RASs are uniform across the Bank. Furthermore, RASs are required to have the same level of quality and follow the same processing as non-RAS ESW/ TA. RAS related activities are also programmed within the CAS/CPS and guidelines have already been developed to define when a RAS should be undertaken (see the Op Memo-The Provision of Reimbursable Advisory Services available on the OPCS website).

These changes help to ensure the balance between RAS versus non-RAS in the Bank's country programs. Third, at completion TTLs/task teams are required to complete a self-assessment of results achieved with greater management oversight. Fourth, this assessment is supplemented with a client feedback instrument administered to both RAS and non-RAS activities. (In fact, the CFI was just completed for the FY12 cohort and the exercise will be launched in the coming months for the FY13 cohort of completed activities). Finally, teams are encouraged to capture/document in Bank systems the evidence of the contribution of their knowledge activity to results achieved.

In addition to the above, a new programmatic instrument for ESW/TA is now on the Ops Portal. Programmatic approaches are encouraged in those situations where they are relevant and appropriate, i.e., in support of medium term reform efforts.

Improving the Results Measurement System for Knowledge Services

IEG FINDINGS & CONCLUSIONS

Bank knowledge services were not monitored and evaluated consistently in the sample of countries. In only 17 percent of the knowledge services assessed was there at least a partial results framework in the CPS, allowing a tracking of the contribution of the activity to the broader development outcomes sought by the CPS. Similarly, only 23 percent of the knowledge services included, at least partly, result indicators to track the achievement of the activity's outcome. Where monitoring and evaluation were better, knowledge services results were more likely to be achieved, most likely reflecting a link between M&E, knowledge services quality, and impact. Implementation and results monitoring systems are needed to track progress toward mutually agreed outcomes and mitigate the risk of fragmentation and loss of strategic focus intrinsic in reimbursable advisory services.

IEG RECOMMENDATIONS

Improving the results measurement system for knowledge services: The Bank should ensure and monitor high-quality results frameworks that respond to client concerns, and link more tightly knowledge services tasks with country partnership strategies milestones and outcome indicators. Use—and continuously improve—implementation results monitoring systems that track progress of knowledge activities towards achieving outcomes in the results framework of the country partnership strategies. Ensure that all knowledge service activities are timely, seek independent validation through systematic pointed client feedback, and use such feedback to assess results and improve results framework of knowledge services. Draw on appropriate evaluation resources and develop tools to evaluate knowledge-based programs.

WB: Agree

MANAGEMENT RESPONSE

WB: Management has already begun to address the issues raised by IEG. As noted above, knowledge services are now more closely linked to outcomes defined at the level of the CPS/CASs. The Bank has strengthened its results framework for knowledge services and is now putting in place processing steps and guidelines to support monitoring and quality. The self-assessment process has been strengthened to have more management oversight. A client feedback instrument is now in operation. The next step is for the Bank to learn from the exercise and use it to inform the automation of the process. This work is now ongoing.

Going forward, the Bank will put in place an approach for ex-post assessment of knowledge work. In that regard, as plans for automation of the CFI proceed, we look forward to working with IEG on developing a framework for ex-post evaluation which covers the full group of client facing knowledge products and internal knowledge products, i.e., ESW/TA, IE, TE and KP. IEG has already initiated this work with a focus on ESW/TA and we expect, as an initial step, to have a framework along with advice on how to strengthen the information content of the Ops Portal to ensure adequate information for decision making, monitoring and ex-post evaluation in the first quarter of FY14.

Staff Incentives for Excellence in Knowledge Services

IEG FINDINGS & CONCLUSIONS

Enhancing the Bank Group's success rate on knowledge services will require that the highest-caliber staff have incentives to be in the knowledge services "business". There is a perception at the Bank that lending experience is essential for promotion, and the performance management system does not have enough incentives to promote knowledge activities. Moreover, country unit budgets are organized around the supervision and execution of lending operations, with knowledge services being in support of such operations. Otherwise, knowledge services are more like incidental items in the operation of country units.

IEG RECOMMENDATIONS

Staff incentives for excellence in knowledge services: Design appropriate incentives to promote staff engagement in knowledge activities. Move to a financial and budget framework that balances managerial incentives for lending and knowledge activities. Link funding to country units to results from country partnership strategy monitoring framework rather than lending operations.

ACCEPTANCE BY MANAGEMENT OF RECOMMENDATION

WB: Partially Agree

MANAGEMENT RESPONSE

WB: Various actions have been initiated to achieve greater incentives for knowledge work. The increased focus on results, client feedback and ex-post evaluation coupled with the improved management oversight (from senior management down to the task team) will help to place greater focus on results. Aside from the changes outlined above, we have instituted a routine management meeting chaired by the managing director and attended by the regional operations directors/vice presidents and the network vice presidents), to jointly review the knowledge and lending portfolio. Starting from FY14, results from the client feedback will be linked to or inform the MOU established between the managing director and the various vice presidents (Regions and networks).

The allocation of resources to support knowledge products is already driven by the country program's expected results. Client and Bank teams determine what outcomes the Bank hopes to influence and then identify the activities needed to achieve these outcomes. Resources are then allocated to support the required activities. In many cases these are stand alone knowledge products that are unrelated to lending.

Management is committed to continue to strengthen and align incentives — including budget — to achieve excellence in knowledge services, and, in general, to achieve improved development results. However, it cannot commit at this stage to specific budget allocation principles, at the time when the entire budget process is being reviewed to align it to the new World Bank Group strategy under development.

Chairperson's Summary:
Committee on Development Effectiveness

On June 24, 2013, the Committee on Development Effectiveness (CODE) met to discuss *Knowledge-Based Country Programs: An Evaluation of World Bank Group Experience* and the *Draft Management Response*.

Summary

The Committee welcomed both the Independent Evaluation Group's (IEG) evaluation — which assessed knowledge-based activities in nine country programs selected from 48 knowledge-intensive programs supported by the World Bank Group — and management's draft response. Members also appreciated the constructive engagement between IEG and management. The Committee agreed with the recommendations and findings, including that relevance to client concerns, technical quality of results, and reference to local policy context drive successful knowledge services; programmatic approaches and consistent engagement achieve better outcomes; stronger results monitoring measures real progress on agreed outcomes; and enhanced staff incentives to promote knowledge activities foster staff commitment. The Committee found the evaluation timely and useful in the context of the ongoing conversation on the Bank's knowledge work, particularly on how knowledge is positioned within the institution's overall strategy in the medium and longer term. Members noted that a core determinant of the Bank's development effectiveness is the extent to which it can combine lending with knowledge and, hence, achieve results and find solutions. In this regard, members underscored that the Bank needs to ensure that knowledge services are more impactful on development outcomes at the country level — and hence, management must promote appropriate staff incentives in respect of knowledge work.

Members noted IEG's findings that results were very similar for free services and Reimbursable Advisory Services (RAS). Yet regardless of the type of knowledge service the Bank provides, members agreed that there needs to be clarity on the objective of a knowledge engagement in a client country, on the value it adds, and on the results framework that underpins its work. This would necessitate a clear understanding between the Bank and the client to ensure knowledge services are aligned appropriately. While it was recognized that RAS is a small part of the Bank's knowledge services, members reinforced that the institution's engagement in RAS should be in line with its overall strategy for a country. Members asked management to ensure the appropriate criteria are in place.

Members appreciated that Bank management intends to continue to strengthen and align staff incentives to achieve excellence in knowledge services. Members acknowledged that management agreed in principle with the recommendation to move to a budget framework that better balances incentives for lending and knowledge activities, but accepted that management could not commit to specifics at this time since the budget process is under review to align it to the new World Bank Group strategy.

Anna Brandt
CHAIRPERSON

1 Introduction

CHAPTER HIGHLIGHTS

- World Bank country programs have shifted toward more intensive delivery of knowledge services relative to lending in the FY05–11 period compared to FY98–04.

- Differences in income levels and external financing requirements appear to be associated with the relative increase of knowledge services in country programs in the top half of a ranking of relative preponderance of knowledge services.

- There is only a weak correlation between the relative Advisory Services intensity of International Finance Corporation (IFC) programs and the knowledge services content of World Bank programs because, while many countries tend to rely less on the Bank's financing as they grow, opportunities for IFC investments may increase along with the size of the market and economic development.

- Selected knowledge activities in the focus countries of the evaluation have been assessed against the criteria of relevance, technical quality, results achieved, and the sustainability of results.

Since the 1990s, the World Bank Group and its country clients have become increasingly cognizant of the importance of knowledge in development. In response to countries' changing needs, the Bank Group has adapted its approach, governance, business practices, and strategic vision. It rebalanced its services away from a predominant focus on finance, toward more effective use of country experiences and global knowledge to meet client needs. The Bank repositioned itself in 1996, through the Knowledge Bank concept, with the aim of enhancing the technical quality of lending services, while developing new streams of knowledge services. This was followed in 1997 by the reorganization of the institution in a matrix management system—which was seen as a more effective means of leveraging the Bank's global knowledge, its sector technical know-how, and its country-specific expertise gained from lending and policy advice.[1] The past decade saw a growth in the knowledge services the Bank provided. According to *Knowledge for Development 2011*, in FY10 the Bank allocated $606 million, or 31 percent of its administrative budget, for core knowledge services, up from 24 percent in FY02.[2] With its Advisory Services operations, the International Finance Corporation (IFC) fulfills a dual role too as a provider of finance to the private sector and knowledge conveyor. IFC's expenditures on Advisory Services increased from $299 million in FY08 to $365 million in FY12.[3]

In parallel, in the decade leading up to the 2008–09 global financial crisis, most of the Bank Group's country clients faced an exceptionally favorable economic environment. Thus, several countries found that they needed less Bank financing, while others—especially new European Union (EU) members from Eastern and Central Europe—graduated from the World Bank's financial assistance. However, most of these countries maintained a partnership with the Bank Group, based on economic and sector work (ESW) and on non-lending technical assistance (TA). Knowledge services have become a more important platform for the Bank to advise these countries on their development agendas. At the same time, arrangements for Reimbursable Advisory Services (RAS) have become more prominent in the Bank's partnerships with country clients.[4] The growing volume of RAS signals that drawing on the Bank's knowledge provides value.

Relative Intensity of Knowledge Services in World Bank Country Programs

Multiple activities generate knowledge at the World Bank Group either as freestanding services or as knowledge embedded in lending operations. Although accurate estimates are difficult to come by, as noted in *Knowledge for Development 2011*, an estimated 10 percent of loan proceeds from projects financed by the Bank are being spent by borrowers on knowledge products that are similar to core knowledge services delivered through the Bank's knowledge services.[5] Henceforth, knowledge products will refer to ESW and TA.

Depending on the intensity of use of knowledge services, Bank programs with country clients can be characterized as evolving along a continuum from programs dominated by finance and relatively lower intensity of knowledge services (lending-based programs, or LBPs) to programs with high knowledge content—where knowledge-based activities are at the core of the relationship (knowledge-based programs, or KBPs). However, drawing a line between KBPs and LBPs is arbitrary. First, the Bank typically offers a mix of lending and knowledge services to its country clients. This mix evolves over time, depending on country economic development and specific circumstances that may generate high or low external financing needs. Second, since knowledge is also generated by lending operations, it is difficult to assess whether a KBP generates more knowledge transfers to clients than an LBP with a country services budget of similar size without more detailed analysis. Subject to these caveats, a working definition of KBPs has been established for this evaluation with the use of indicators that help categorize World Bank country programs according to the predominance of knowledge services. Four indicators have been used (box 1.1):

- The number of Bank lending operations in proportion to the number of knowledge products;

- Resources allocated to Bank lending operations (cost of project preparation and supervision) in proportion to resources allocated to knowledge products;

- Resources allocated to knowledge products as a percentage of country

- services budget; and

- The number of knowledge products delivered.

Thus, abstracting from the knowledge services incorporated in lending operations, the lower the value of the first two indicators and the higher the value of the last two, the higher the knowledge content of country programs. Using these four indicators, a comparison of the periods FY05–11 and FY98–04 reveals a shift of Bank country programs toward more intensive delivery of knowledge services relative to lending (figure 1.1).

A ranking of 138 World Bank country programs based on the relative knowledge content (relative use of ESW and TA) over FY05–11 was established using the average of the country program scores on each of the four indicators (appendix A). A descriptive analysis of the 138 country programs categorized—in decreasing order—in terciles of the distribution of relative knowledge intensity shows that there are significant differences in the mix of Bank services among the three terciles (Table 1.1). Countries with programs categorized in the upper third of relative knowledge intensity had, on average, per capita GDP 2.5 times higher than countries in the other two terciles—among which there was no significant difference in per capita

World Bank knowledge services and knowledge activities covered in this report consist of economic sector work (ESW) and technical assistance (TA). International Finance Corporation (IFC) activities are Advisory Services where the government was a client. Knowledge activities were selected in consultation with country management units, paying attention to links to strategic priorities in country partnership strategies. The selection of countries that included IFC Advisory Services was designed to illustrate complementarities and synergies with the Bank in those countries. The recommendations in this report are intended to apply to countries similar to those in the sample, and the small size of IFC Advisory Services reviewed does not provide a full illustration of IFC Advisory Service effectiveness. Note that given the sample of projects drawn on is relatively small in the case of IFC, the findings and recommendations should be taken to be most relevant to the World Bank's knowledge work with some global applicability to the Bank group but not IFC specifically.

Bank country programs were selected according to the preponderance of knowledge services using the following criteria: ratio of number of lending projects to number of knowledge activities, ratio of lending cost to knowledge service cost, share of knowledge services cost in country services budget, and number of knowledge activities. The combination of criteria intends to eliminate biases of any one criterion taken individually. Lending continues to play a crucial role in many middle-income countries, and this evaluation does not suggest that a linear transition from lending to knowledge services is the desired pathway for a given country.

Two broad program categories with preponderance of knowledge services were distinguished:

• Programs in countries where there is no pressing need for Bank financing and the partnership is thus designed with a strong focus on knowledge services.

• Programs in countries where the Bank's involvement revolves around non-lending activities because there is an insufficient foundation for a reform-oriented lending program.

To assign countries with preponderance of knowledge services to one of the two categories, the evaluation used Country Policy and Institutional Assessment (CPIA) ratings over calendar years 2004–10. Countries with below-average CPIA ratings were put in the second category and removed from the sample. Focus was placed on the first half along a continuum of relative preponderance of knowledge services, with 48 countries fitting a working definition of knowledge-based programs. Additional criteria to narrow down the set of countries:

continued on next page

- **Primary criterion:** upper-middle-income countries by per capita income level over 2005–10.

- **Secondary criteria** to include countries:
    - mostly toward the high end of the knowledge services preponderance continuum
    - with diversified economic structure
    - with above-average size of knowledge services program
    - with no Bank lending services
    - with significant (average or above-average) use of Bank lending services
    - with fee-based services
    - that are Organisation for Economic Co-operation and Development members or new European Union members.

- The selected focus countries are Bulgaria, Chile, China, Kazakhstan, Kuwait, Malaysia, the Russian Federation, South Africa, and Thailand.

FIGURE 1.1 Lending and Knowledge Activities in World Bank Country Programs (FY98–04 versus FY05–11)

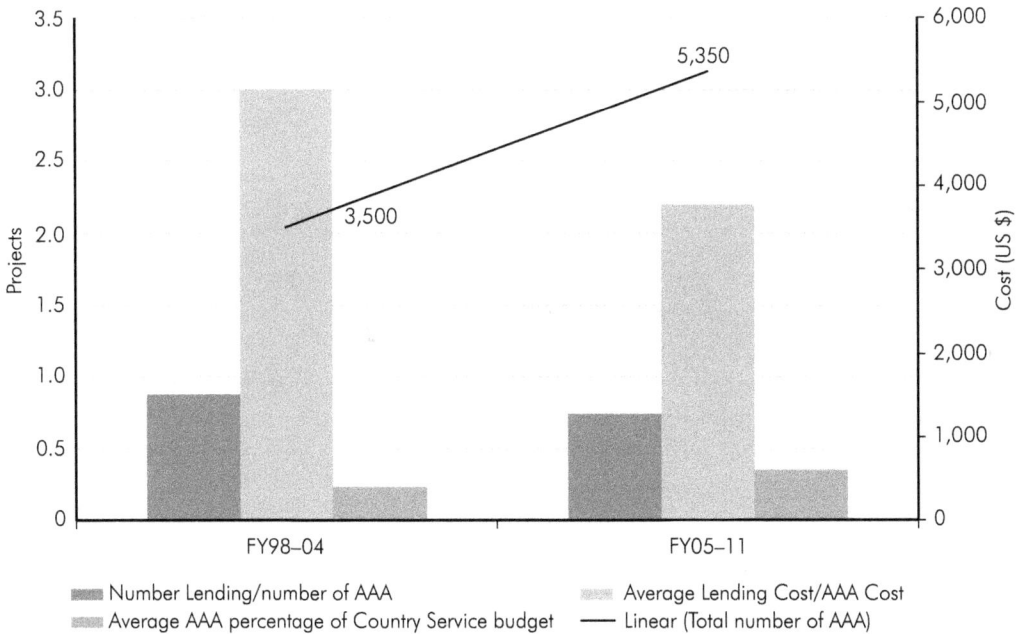

SOURCE: World Bank Business Warehouse data.

NOTE: AAA = analytical and advisory activities.

TABLE 1.1 Selected Corporate and Economic Indicators Associated with World Bank Country Programs Categorized According to the Relative Intensity of Knowledge Services (FY05–11)

Corporate and economic indicators	Percentile of the continuum of relative knowledge		
	Upper-third percentile	Middle-third percentile	Lower-third percentile
Average number of lending operations/number of knowledge products	0.3	0.7	1.2
Average resources for lending/knowledge services resources	0.8	2.0	3.5
Average knowledge services resources as percentage of country service budget	54.4	30.7	21.4
Number of knowledge products	2,144	2,224	982
Number of knowledge products as percentage of total Bank knowledge products	40.1	41.6	18.4
Average number of knowledge products by country	48.7	49.4	20.0
Total lending commitments (millions of US$)	70,728	130,011	47,945
Lending commitments as percentage of total Bank lending commitments	28.4	52.3	19.3
GDP per capita (in constant 2007 PPP US$, average over calendar years 2005–10)	12,683	4,840	4,703
Current account balance (as percentage of GDP, average over calendar years 2005–10)	0.8	−6.7	−5.1

SOURCES: World Bank data and World Development Indicators.
NOTE: GDP = gross domestic product; PPP = purchasing power parity.

income. Countries in the upper third had, on average, a small current account surplus over 2005–10, compared to deficits of 6.7 and 5 percent of GDP in the middle and lower third of the distribution. Differences in income levels and external financing requirements are thus, probably, a driver of the higher mix of knowledge services relative to finance in the country

TABLE 1.2 IFC Advisory Services and Investment Operations Associated with World Bank Country Programs According to Their Relative Knowledge Service Content (FY05–11)

Indicators	Percentile on the continuum of relative knowledge service intensity of World Bank country programs		
	Upper-third percentile	Middle-third percentile	Lower-third percentile
Average number of IFC Advisory Services	13.0	16.6	5.7
Average number of IFC investment operations	17.0	24.4	9.6
Investment operations/Advisory Services	1.9	2.0	2.1

SOURCE: World Bank Business Warehouse data.

programs in the upper third of the distribution. RAS for knowledge services were present in 16 of the 44 countries in the upper third, accounting on average for 50 percent of country services budgets for these countries (appendix A). On the other hand, reimbursement was present in only four countries in the middle third and three in the lower third.

In contrast, the patterns of IFC Advisory Services relative to investments are different from the patterns of Bank knowledge services intensity to lending. When IFC Advisory Services and investment operations are classified according to the continuum of knowledge services intensity of World Bank country programs, there is only a weak correlation between the Advisory Services intensity of IFC programs and the knowledge content of World Bank programs. In the upper third of knowledge intensive World Bank programs, IFC delivered, on average, 1.9 investment operations in proportion to Advisory Services. This proportion was only marginally higher in countries in the medium and lower thirds of the knowledge services intensity continuum of Bank programs (table 1.2). IFC's mix of Advisory Services and investments was thus practically invariant along the relative knowledge services continuum of Bank country programs. One reason is that, while many of the World Bank's country clients tend to rely less on the Bank's financing and more on its knowledge services as they grow, opportunities for IFC investments may increase along with the size of the market and economic development. At the same time, with the improvement of the quality of regulations in countries with robust private sectors, the scope for IFC Advisory Services may decrease. To further complicate matters, the funding of IFC Advisory Services by donor trust funds may shape the allocation of services toward specific countries or regions, not closely related to patterns of economic development.

Objectives, Scope, and Methodology of the Evaluation

As a growing number of emerging market economies rely less on World Bank financing, opportunities for Bank knowledge transfers to clients through lending have declined. Despite the spike in lending during the 2008–09 global financial crisis, opportunities for knowledge transfers through lending are likely to diminish further in the future, especially in upper-middle-income countries with no pressing financing needs or with improving access to diversified sources of finance. The Bank's ability to contribute to development policy and poverty reduction through finance may thus become more limited. Knowledge-based country programs in upper-middle-income countries will therefore become a more important platform for the Bank to advise clients on their development agendas.

The objective of this evaluation is to learn lessons from diverse practices in the World Bank's knowledge-based programs with high (Kuwait) and upper-middle-income countries, to help leverage the Bank's global knowledge most effectively to meet the needs of these countries that are not in pressing need of finance and mainly rely on knowledge services.

Some key questions the evaluation will answer in pursuing this objective are the following:

• How best can the Bank Group maintain its relevance in knowledge-based partnerships?

• How does the World Bank position itself as a development partner of choice in upper-middle-income countries?

• What are the success factors for knowledge services to achieve expected results?

• How can the World Bank add more value for clients through appropriate scope and instruments of knowledge-based country programs?

Over the past few years, the Independent Evaluation Group (IEG) has conducted three evaluations that address some aspects of knowledge services provided by the Bank Group: *Development Results in Middle-Income Countries: An Evaluation of the World Bank's Support* (in 2007); *Using Knowledge to Improve Development Effectiveness: An Evaluation of World Bank Economic and Sector Work and Technical Assistance, 2000–2006* (in 2008), and *Independent Evaluation of IFC's Development Results: Knowledge for Private Sector Development* (in 2009)—see Box 1.2. This evaluation fills a gap in previous work because it assesses the performance of knowledge services in the context of country programs that revolve primarily around such services.

As the primary objective of the evaluation is to understand how the World Bank can most effectively work with country clients that do not rely on Bank financing, and as IFC's engagement through Advisory Services follows a different pattern from the World Bank's

BOX 1.2 Previous IEG Evaluations of Knowledge Services

The main recommendations of the three evaluations of knowledge services conducted by the Independent Evaluation Group (IEG) are as follows:

Development Results in Middle-Income Countries: An Evaluation of the World Bank's Support

- Draw on country capacity and develop each country's own expertise

- Demonstrate best practice in its support to countries

- Increase the Bank's agility in support of countries

- Make the most of cooperation across the Bank, International Finance Corporation (IFC), and the Multilateral Investment Guarantee Agency (MIGA) to successfully offer clients a more effective package from its combined resources.

Using Knowledge to Improve Development Effectiveness: An Evaluation of World Bank Economic and Sector Work and Technical Assistance, 2000–2006

- Reinvigorate the Bank's mandate to maintain a strong knowledge base

- Ensure that ESW tasks in countries funded by the International Development Association (IDA) are adequately resourced, even if it means fewer economic and sector work (ESW) tasks in some countries

- Enhance the institutional arrangements for undertaking ESW and technical assistance by ensuring substantive task team presence in country offices, particularly in countries with low institutional capacity, and by formulating a dissemination strategy at the concept paper stage

- Build on client preferences, including clients' feedback after completing the task

- Take the results tracking framework seriously.

Independent Evaluation of IFC's Development Results: Knowledge for Private Sector Development

- Effectively manage the tension between protecting the portfolio and responding to opportunities during the crisis

- Set out a clear vision and business framework for Advisory Services that is more closely linked with IFC's global corporate strategy

- Pursue more programmatic Advisory Services interventions

- Over the long term, pricing of Advisory Services should reflect the value and impact (that is, not just the cost)

- Strengthen Advisory Services performance measurement and internal knowledge management.

KBPs, lessons learned are not applicable to IFC. However, the evaluation aims to draw lessons on how best the synergy between the Bank's knowledge services and IFC Advisory Services could be mutually reinforced in promoting private sector development in upper-middle-income countries with Bank KBPs. These lessons are not intended as a comprehensive assessment of IFC-World Bank synergy but rather of the way that synergy plays out in countries with knowledge-based World Bank programs.

To deliver on its objective, the evaluation uses focus countries selected from among the countries that make relatively more intensive use of the Bank's core knowledge services. The selected countries are Bulgaria, Chile, China, Kazakhstan, Kuwait, Malaysia, the Russian Federation, South Africa, and Thailand. The evaluation has also taken into account IFC Advisory Services in China, Kazakhstan, the Russian Federation, and South Africa. The nine selected countries are high (Kuwait) and upper-middle-income countries with a high share of knowledge services in their programs. They were selected to include countries with a diversified economic structure, countries with an above average size of knowledge services program, countries with no Bank lending, countries with fee-based knowledge services, and countries which are Organisation for Economic Co-operation and Development (OECD) or new EU members. The selection was designed to provide useful illustrations of knowledge service effectiveness in the selected countries, not to provide a sample for statistical projection to overall knowledge service assistance to those countries or the full set of Bank clients. Furthermore, the selection of countries that included IFC Advisory Services was designed to illustrate complementarities and synergies with the Bank in those countries, not to provide a full illustration of IFC Advisory Services effectiveness in those countries.

The World Bank delivered 751 knowledge products to the focus countries over FY05–11 while IFC delivered 185 Advisory Service projects to both private and government entities over the same period—see Table 1.3 for a breakdown of Bank knowledge services by thematic areas.[6] Approximately three-quarters of all knowledge services were delivered in the areas of private sector, infrastructure and economic policy, and public sector governance. There is wide variation among the countries in the distribution of knowledge services across sectors. For example, while Infrastructure represents 39 percent of knowledge services in China, it represents approximately 10 percent in Malaysia. And whereas private sector constitutes 51 percent of the knowledge services in Kuwait, it represents 16 percent in Malaysia and Thailand. The variation observed in the distribution of knowledge services reflects different country priorities.

In view of the large number of knowledge products delivered by Bank programs in the focus countries, the evaluation uses a purposely selected sample of knowledge products delivered over FY05–11. The criteria used to select the knowledge products and IFC Advisory Services

TABLE 1.3 Distribution of Bank Knowledge Services and IFC Advisory Services across Countries and Thematic Sectors (FY05–11)

Country	Agriculture (%)	Education/health (%)	Private sector (%)	Infra-structure (%)	Economic policy/ public sector governance (%)	Poverty reduction/ social protection (%)	All knowledge services (number)	Sample knowledge services (number)	All IFC Advisory Services (number)	Sample IFC Advisory Services (number)
Bulgaria	5.1	5.1	25.6	28.2	25.4	10.3	39	18	5	0
Chile	4.1	26.5	28.6	10.2	22.4	8.2	49	25	2	0
China	9.8	6.3	18.5	39.0	17.6	8.8	205	50	70	13
Kazakhstan	3.1	7.0	29.7	11.7	37.5	10.9	128	49	5	4
Kuwait	–	9.8	51.2	14.6	24.4	–	41	15	0	0
Malaysia	3.2	16.1	16.1	9.7	54.8	–	31	13	0	0
Russian Federation	8.6	14.8	18.8	24.2	18.8	14.8	128	49	71	9
South Africa	12.5	5.4	26.8	28.6	23.2	3.6	56	21	26	8
Thailand	–	16.2	16.2	18.9	32.4	16.2	74	26	6	0
All AAA (%)	6.3	10.7	23.6	24.1	25.7	9.7	–	–	–	–
All (number)	47	80	177	181	193	73	751	–	185	–
Sample (%)	7.5	11.7	32.7	9.0	26.3	12.8	–	–	–	–
Sample (number)	20	31	87	24	70	34	–	266	–	34

NOTE: AAA = analytical and advisory activities; – = data not available.

are described in Appendix B. The sample includes 266 World Bank knowledge products and 34 IFC Advisory Service projects (see table 1.3). In order to capture activity synergies and possible complementary results, selected knowledge products and IFC Advisory Services were grouped, whenever possible, into "knowledge activities" with similar objectives or thematic focus. Thus, the sample of Bank knowledge services was reduced from 266 to 196 activities and the sample of IFC Advisory Services was reduced from 34 to 32 activities. Therefore, the number of "knowledge activities" reviewed by this evaluation is 228. The list of the "knowledge activities" reviewed and the underlying knowledge products and IFC Advisory

Services is in Appendix B. As with the selection of countries, the selection of knowledge was intended to illustrate knowledge service effectiveness and synergies, not to project results statistically to the full range of Bank knowledge services and Bank/IFC Advisory Services synergies of knowledge services in the selected countries. The selected knowledge activities in the nine focus countries have been assessed against four criteria:

- *Relevance* is intended to assess the extent to which the knowledge activities were suited to the priority needs of the recipients and to the achievement of key development goals of the country client

- *Technical quality* of the knowledge activities and their effectiveness in leveraging the Bank's global knowledge and conveying relevant and customized expertise to recipients

- *Results* are intended to assess whether the knowledge activities attained their objectives, whether results can be traced and attributed to the Bank, and whether the process through which the knowledge services were delivered and shared with various stakeholders supported the achievement of results

- *Sustainability of results* as a measure of whether the knowledge activities are likely to have lasting impacts (on policies, capacity, or institutions) after their completion, and whether an appropriate framework is in place to monitor results over time.

This review is not meant to be a full-fledged evaluation of country program performance. As in most focus countries the review was conducted while the most recently approved knowledge-based country programs was under implementation, prior to the completion of their cycle, and covered only a subset of the knowledge services completed under the country programs.

IEG has conducted evaluation of knowledge services in various areas, beyond the Bank's lending operations, building on the knowledge service assessment methodology used by the Bank's Quality Assurance Group (QAG). The methodology applicable to knowledge services has been tested by IEG in thematic evaluations.[7] This evaluation draws on IEG's assessment methodology for knowledge services, with appropriate modifications. The evaluation template for the selected knowledge activities was designed to reflect the four assessment criteria (Appendix F). The necessary information was collected by the evaluation team through desk reviews of country partnership strategies and project documents and through interviews with Bank staff, government officials, and other stakeholders, including representatives from civil society organizations.

The report is organized in five chapters including the present chapter. Chapter 2 reviews the relevance and strategic positioning of the World Bank in knowledge-based partnerships.

Chapter 3 reviews the technical quality of the knowledge services delivered. Chapter 4 evaluates the results of the knowledge activities and their sustainability, as well as the synergy between World Bank knowledge services and IFC Advisory Services in promoting private and financial sector development. Chapter 5 draws conclusions and discusses the lessons learned from the evaluation.

Endnotes

[1] The Bank has continued to improve its internal organization for knowledge management, and is presently engaged in a reinvigoration of the peer review process to improve the quality of knowledge products.

[2] "Core knowledge services" include economic and sector work (ESW) and technical assistance (TA) for external clients, knowledge services produced as a public good, and analytical work for internal use.

[3] International Finance Corporation (IFC) Annual Reports, FY06, FY08, and FY12.

[4] Over FY06–11 Reimbursable Advisory Services grew from $12.2 million to $30.6 million.

[5] Such "knowledge flows from operations" were estimated by the *Independent Evaluation of IFC's Development Results: Knowledge for Private Sector Development* study at $2.5 billion in FY11, far outstripping the estimated amount of core Bank knowledge services ($606 million, of which $444 million was for external clients).

[6] Infrastructure includes energy and mining, environment, transport, and urban development. Poverty reduction/social protection also includes social development. Private sector includes private and financial sector and financial management.

[7] The Independent Evaluation Group (IEG) conducted an evaluation of World Bank ESW and TA in 2008 (*Using Knowledge to Improve Development Effectiveness: An Evaluation of World Bank Economic and Sector Work and Technical Assistance, 2000–2006*). An evaluation of growth diagnostics in Africa was conducted in 2010 (*Performance Assessment Review, World Bank Economic Reports on Growth Diagnostics in Four African Countries: Ghana, Mauritius, Nigeria, and Uganda*), followed by an evaluation of AAA on Revenue Policy (*World Bank Support for Revenue Policy Reform in Eastern Europe and Central Asia: Performance Assessment Reports of ESW in Georgia, Kazakhstan and Kyrgyz Republic*) and a clustered evaluation of investment climate assessments in emerging economies (*Performance Assessment Review of Investment Climate Assessments in Five Transforming Economies: Bangladesh, Egypt, Guatemala, Kenya, and Vietnam*).

2

Relevance of the World Bank in Knowledge-Based Partnerships

CHAPTER HIGHLIGHTS

- In most of the focus countries there was a structured partnership for the delivery of the World Bank's knowledge-based program, although in some cases there was no results framework.

- In a majority of World Bank knowledge services and IFC Advisory Services reviewed, the issues addressed were relevant to the client, while the design of the activities was appropriate to meet their objectives.

- In more than a quarter of knowledge services and Advisory Services, however, there were issues pertinent to the client that the activities were at least partly unable to address—when reports provided very broad suggestions, with lack of customized solutions aligned with the clients' demands.

- The knowledge services delivered by the Bank Group have had multiple uses, with raising stakeholder awareness being predominant. Client participation was generally high—an indication of client interest and relevance of the work conducted.

- Full dissemination of Bank knowledge services was conducted in slightly more than half of knowledge services reviewed. The confidentiality often imposed on Bank knowledge services cofinanced by clients or through Reimbursable Advisory Services (RAS) has lowered the rate of dissemination of Bank knowledge services.

- Key strengths of the Bank's knowledge services acknowledged by counterparts include the ability of benchmarking against good practice, reputation and credibility, ability to customize to the local context, and capacity to deliver multisector development solutions.

- The Bank's recognized capacity to customize and deliver multisector solutions, however, might be challenged when there is insufficient knowledge products to gain appropriate depth and breadth of country knowledge.

- There are some good examples where the Bank's knowledge services facilitated South-South exchanges, but more can be done as the Bank's geographic, thematic, and organizational fragmentation prevents realizing the full potential of such exchanges.

- The Bank's positioning as a strategic partner and policy advisor with respect to other knowledge providers is generally favorable.

This chapter assesses whether the Bank Group has remained relevant in countries with knowledge-based World Bank country programs and how it is positioning itself in countries that make relatively little use of its financial services. The chapter first assesses the overall fit of knowledge-based country programs with the development challenges of these countries and looks at the relevance of the design of the knowledge services delivered. Next, it looks at the relevance of the knowledge services delivered from the perspective of their use and the extent of client participation in the activities. Finally, it assesses how clients perceive the strengths and weaknesses of knowledge services delivered by the Bank Group in the focus countries and what it means for the strategic positioning of the Bank Group with respect to other providers of knowledge and advice.

Fit of World Bank Knowledge-Based Country Programs with Country Challenges

Despite diminishing financing needs of several focus countries, owing to strong growth and the accumulation of substantial financial buffers (Chile, China, Kazakhstan, Kuwait, Malaysia, and the Russian Federation) or access to other sources of financing, such as European Union (EU) structural funds (Bulgaria), overall, the Bank has maintained strong engagement through a change in country partnerships toward knowledge services. The World Bank faces multiple client demands for knowledge services in these countries and, to remain relevant, responds with different products, delivery practices, and under various financing arrangements. In several cases, International Finance Corporation (IFC) Advisory Services respond to similar client demands and often complement the Bank's knowledge activities. Based on the Independent Evaluation Group's (IEG's) review of World Bank knowledge services in the focus countries, client demand generally falls into four categories:

- Customized development solutions

- Experience sharing and innovative ideas

- Capacity development

- Public knowledge goods.

Customized development solutions. These are studies or technical assistance (TA)—delivered mostly as Reimbursable Advisory Services (RAS)—that fill knowledge gaps in areas where counterparts need to develop a strategy or to take action. Relevance, timeliness, and customized advice through actionable recommendations are seen by counterparts as key. Such was the case in Chile, with TA on the management of financial resources of the pension fund or with studies on quality assurance in education and the program of student loans. In Bulgaria, the Bank's new partnership provides customized policy support for the implementation of the Europe 2020 strategy and for accelerated absorption of EU funds. In the Russian Federation, there is a growing demand for the Bank's global knowledge for development solutions at the subnational level. At the same time, IFC provided advice on how to improve business access to land by using knowledge generated from regional surveys. In China, where knowledge services are being delivered along with a sizable lending program, counterparts sought the Bank's advice for solutions to specific problems—such as a rural health system and energy-efficient transport system, based not only on rigorous analysis but also on demonstrations of their applicability to China through pilot lending projects. In parallel, IFC helped draft the personal bankruptcy law, design the credit reporting system, and develop a modern secured transaction systems. While based on experience in other countries, these initiatives had to be designed to take into account the Chinese context, including the state of current institutions and attitudes.

Experience sharing and innovative ideas. The Bank faces strong demand for studies or seminars that explore issues in an area where counterparts have not taken a position and where the Bank functions as a "sounding board" or connects counterparts to cutting-edge international expertise through its broadly recognized convening power. IFC also faces similar demands for Advisory Services intended to share IFC experience and global knowledge or demonstrate the feasibility of a solution to a policy issue. In Kazakhstan, the Joint Economic Research Program (JERP) is anchored in policy analysis, good practice options notes, and brainstorming sessions with high-level officials on a variety of topics where the government needs to form a view. The brainstorming sessions have become a critical platform to share opinion and help the authorities systematically think through issues with substantial analytical support from the Bank. In Bulgaria, the Bank's knowledge services often served to validate the government's views and have been used, in particular by the Ministry of Finance, to strengthen the dialogue with line ministries. This was the case in Chile as well, with Bank reports on policy assessment lessons from Organisation for Economic Co-operation and Development (OECD) countries or on decentralization. In some cases, there is a high sensitivity to embracing Bank policy recommendations due to political economy considerations, as, for example, in South Africa, especially on labor issues.

In Malaysia, the requests reflected a desire on the part of the client for the Bank to provide the intellectual underpinning, through theoretical and empirical evidence, for policy measures that had been debated internally. Studies addressed key aspects of building a high-income economy—raising productivity, increasing the added value of industry, improving equality, improving corporate governance, and raising standards. China also looked to the Bank for new concepts, advanced methodologies, and modern practices in formulating its own long-term strategies. Such advice tended to be provided either in the form of high-profile reports, such as China 2030 and the Guangdong Reducing Inequality knowledge product, or as informal policy notes destined for a small circle of policy makers. In parallel, with the government's focus on regional development, IFC helped introduce in Sichuan province several best practices and techniques in the area of investment promotion, such as use of cluster and value chain analysis. Successful demonstration of these practices in Sichuan would provide other regions with investment promotion models to consider. In the Russian Federation, the Bank delivered knowledge services on economic diversification, competition, and innovation at a time when these topics were not on the agenda of policy makers. At the same time, the World Bank and IFC jointly developed the subnational Doing Business Survey and monitoring system targeted toward the specific needs of local governments. The authorities intend to use the indicators for evaluating regional performance.

Capacity development. Very often the client is interested in knowledge that helps build capacity through training, networking, or access to international best practices. This service is typically delivered in the form of RAS, but not always. Such demand was strong in South Africa, with RAS for land reform but also TA for macroeconomic modeling. There are multiple examples of TA for capacity development in the focus countries: for risk-based pension and insurance supervision in Chile; for risk-based tax audits, the analysis of tax incidence and for anticorruption in Thailand; for performance-based budgeting in the Russian Federation and Bulgaria; and on regional innovation systems and best practices in nurturing innovation in enterprises in the Russian Federation. IFC also responded through Advisory Services to similar capacity development demands: to investment promotion agencies in two earthquake-affected provinces in China on how to restore the flow of private investments and speed economic recovery; to several private sector–run entrepreneurship programs in South Africa, including one that focused on women entrepreneurs. IFC's South Africa work on pilot credit bureaus, focusing on microfinance clients, is being replicated by the private sector, with the Bankers' Association planning to embark on similar schemes. IFC used experience from other countries to design a project that addressed risks emanating from negative attitudes toward information sharing.

Public knowledge goods. In addition to these services overwhelmingly driven by client demand, in all focus countries the Bank provided knowledge services as public goods (see box 2.1), typically fully funded by the Bank. These include Financial Sector Assessment Program (FSAP) reports in several countries and Reports on the Observance of Standards and Codes (ROSCs) with frequent focus on corporate governance and accounting and auditing. Investment Climate Assessments (ICAs) have been very much in demand in almost all focus countries of the evaluation. Regularly published Economic Monitoring Reports are another

Bank knowledge services primarily driven by client demand typically respond to needs at different stages of the policy-making process in a given area the client is considering, from looking into global experience ("experience sharing and innovative ideas"), through designing an approach or strategy ("customized development solutions"), and to implementing strategies ("capacity development"). In addition, the Bank provides "public knowledge" services not driven by those immediate client needs and usually fully funded by the Bank. For example, Financial Sector Programs, Reports on the Observance of Standards and Codes, or Investment Climate Assessments may not respond to immediate drives to reform the financial sector, corporate governance, or the investment climate, and yet provide broader "public knowledge" that may eventually lead to policies in those areas. Similarly, Economic Monitoring Reports or development policy reviews may cover a range of issues of public interest that extend beyond the focus of current public policy making and serve as tools for broad country-level consultation. These may be relatively more relevant from the broad perspective of country development challenges than from the perspective of the country's more immediate policy focus.

The *Malaysia Economic Monitor* provides an example of such "public knowledge good," where the Bank covers macroeconomic developments and addresses a topical issue following consultation with various stakeholders. The April 2012 issue, for example, covered macroeconomic performance and policies; growth prospects and progress of structural reforms; and a special section on labor markets and policies, including social insurance. Accordingly, the report provides information of broad interest to the public that may eventually feed into policy-making efforts. These knowledge products help the Bank maintain the broad development focus that accounts for much of its appeal to clients.

knowledge product that functions as a public good. In Thailand, the Bank has produced the *Economic Monitor* twice a year for over a decade. The report is broadly disseminated and the Bank conducts regular consultations with the key stakeholders prior to publication. In Malaysia, too, the bank produces the *Economic Monitor* with a macroeconomic update and an analysis of a topical issue. The Bank selects the theme for each publication in consultation with the government, academics, and local think tanks.

The Bank has been working in the focus countries with flexible financing arrangements and delivery mechanisms for knowledge services. Clients often participate in the financing of knowledge work, which indicates that the Bank's knowledge service products are relevant to the clients. In Kuwait, the Bank's knowledge services program is entirely delivered through RAS, as is mostly the case in Malaysia. In both countries, the Bank does not deliver lending services, but there is selective lending in Bulgaria, Chile, Kazakhstan, the Russian Federation, South Africa, and Thailand. In Chile and Kazakhstan, knowledge activities are being designed and delivered through jointly financed programs. In the Russian Federation, the knowledge services program over FY08–11 was funded up to 46 percent through RAS, with a strong focus on knowledge services for regional governments and other nonfederal institutions. In Bulgaria, China, South Africa, and Thailand, knowledge services have been mainly financed through the Bank's administrative budget. In China, in particular, the Bank's country program remained firmly tied to lending, with knowledge services supporting and being supported by lending services. In Bulgaria, a sizeable RAS program is about to be initiated with focus on facilitating Bulgaria's convergence with EU standards through the EU 2020 Strategy.

World Bank knowledge-based country programs typically face a tension between the need for flexibility to respond to rapidly changing client needs and the need for a structured partnership with relevance to the country's development challenges, able to track development results. In eight of the evaluation's nine focus countries there was a structured partnership for the delivery of the World Bank's knowledge-based program. Country partnership strategies (CPSs) in these countries contained strategic pillars aligned with the governments' programs, thus ensuring their overall strategic relevance. The pillars were comprehensive enough to encompass several areas of Bank engagement and the CPS documents highlighted the knowledge and lending services to be provided in each area. In Malaysia, the Bank has not had a CPS since 1999. The Bank entered into a framework agreement with the government in 2009, which defines the legal responsibilities of both parties for largely RAS but does not identify strategic pillars or outcomes. Other countries with knowledge-based World Bank programs not covered by this evaluation, such as Saudi Arabia, also have no formal CPS.

In Thailand, the CPS had not been updated for a long time, with the FY03–05 Country Assistance Strategy (CAS) carried forward through FY10.[1] The centerpiece of the relationship was the Country Development Partnerships (CDPs), revolving around TA and ESW. There was at least one CDP for each of the CAS pillars. The CDPs formed a practical platform for collaboration that allowed Bank interventions to be adjusted to the needs of the moment. In response to the need for flexibility in addressing evolving client demands, the 2004 Kazakhstan CPS was open-ended by design. It was expected to remain in force as long as it remained relevant to the client, provided value added to the country's development process, and addressed the challenges of the policy environment, with a regular progress report assessing CPS relevance against these criteria.

Most CPS documents usually included a results framework with outcome indicators specific to each area of engagement. Results indicators could be elaborate or generic, in the latter case making it difficult to attribute results to the Bank's activities (for example, GDP growth above 5 percent in Chile; preventing real appreciation of the ruble in excess of 7 percent, or keeping federal expenditures below 18 percent of GDP in the Russian Federation). In Thailand, a rather complicated results framework, with measurement, partnership, implementation, and risk elements, was presented in the FY03–05 CAS and intended to be used for each CDP. The framework agreement with Malaysia does not provide a results framework for assessing the impact of the Bank's knowledge services.

More recent CPSs (as, for example, the FY07–11 the Russian Federation CPS, the FY11–13 Bulgaria CPS) have a detailed results framework that links planned knowledge services to specific outcomes expected to be influenced by the Bank's program and provide milestones to track implementation progress. Generally, few measurable indicators to trace progress toward the milestones, and CPS outcomes are being provided. In Kazakhstan, the FY12–17 CPS presents a results framework, including major milestones and outputs and expected outcomes for each priority area in the government's strategy supported by the Bank program. The results framework lists proposed activities in support of each of these outcomes. The new CPS envisions a programmatic approach aimed at strengthening the strategic focus of the JERP. This would be achieved through improving task sequencing, emphasizing interconnected tasks to better address policy linkages, and better tracking of impact.

The CPS is also an important instrument in guiding the selection of IFC Advisory Service projects in a country. In China, projects in access to finance and regional development not only aligned with the CPS but also made a significant contribution to the achievement of expected outcomes. In the Russian Federation, the IFC work on land transactions and markets was part of a program, along with a World Bank investment loan, to achieve one of the stated outcomes in the CPS. In South Africa, IFC focused its projects on micro, small, and medium enterprises (MSME) in line with the CPS emphasis on MSME. In general, the quality of the CPS documents and their results frameworks provide strategic direction to Advisory Services work and enable a more programmatic and longer-term approach to achieve higher development impact than would be the case when project selection is made on an ad hoc and opportunistic basis.

IFC Advisory Service projects would have to be justified based on several criteria articulated in the concept and approval documents.[2] There is no formal coordination mechanism that would enable Bank staff or management to provide inputs to the decision making. In practice, IFC country representatives typically coordinate with World Bank country managers or financial and private sector development staff in the field. A formal coordination mechanism between IFC Advisory Services and Bank knowledge services would help improve alignment of Bank

Group knowledge activities with CPS objectives. For example, the work in South Africa on competition policy and administrative barriers would have benefited from such a mechanism.

In most of the focus countries, especially when the Bank delivered RAS, the content of the program was decided in consultation with the authorities—an indication of its overall relevance to the client. In Chile, the Bank consults with line ministries and other agencies to identify sector priorities but the selection of activities under the Joint Studies Program (JSP) is decided jointly with the Director of Budgets of the Ministry of Finance (DIPRES), which has a strong influence on the content of the JSP. The Bank commits few of its own resources to knowledge services outside of the JSP. Cofinancing of the JSP by the government indicates that the authorities find value in the Bank's knowledge services, which ensures that the knowledge work conducted through the JSP remains relevant as it is demand-driven. In Kazakhstan too, the knowledge-based country program is anchored by the JERP. That program has contributed to increasing the relevance of the Bank work in Kazakhstan.[3] In Malaysia, the requests for reimbursable knowledge services are coordinated by the Economic Planning Unit of the Prime Minister's Department. Seventeen agreements have been concluded since 2009.

Coordination of the knowledge-based program was weaker in Thailand and in South Africa, as knowledge services were provided to various counterparts on demand, sometimes piecemeal, funded by the Bank's budget. However, knowledge activities were aligned with the priorities of the CPSs. Similarly, in the Russian Federation, coordination was comparatively weaker than in other countries as the vast majority of RAS—covering 68 percent of the RAS budget over FY08–11—was delivered to regional governments and other nonfederal institutions.

The relevance of the Bank Group's knowledge services appears to be broadly confirmed by IEG's review of Bank knowledge activities and IFC Advisory Services in the focus countries. The issues addressed in the majority of Bank knowledge activities and IFC Advisory Services reviewed were identified as a development constraint or opportunity, either in the CPS or in previous sector work, lending, or policy dialogue (Table 2.1). The activities reviewed were demand-driven as the client had requested or commissioned the vast majority of Bank knowledge services and most of the IFC Advisory Services. IEG found the design of the majority of reviewed Bank knowledge services and IFC Advisory Services appropriate to meet their objectives, which corroborates their relevance. At the same time, some knowledge services could have been better tailored to client needs. IEG found that in more than a quarter of knowledge services and Advisory Services there were issues relevant to the client that these knowledge activities were at least partly unable to address (Table 2.1).

TABLE 2.1 Relevance Indic of Knowledge and Advisory Services Reviewed by IEG (Percent of Reviewed Activities)

Indicators	Categories	Percentage			
		NA	No	Partly	Yes
Issues addressed by knowledge activity identified as development constraint or opportunity	World Bank Knowledge Services	6.1	12.2	9.7	71.4
	IFC Advisory Services	0	3.1	6.3	90.6
Activity requested by the client	World Bank Knowledge Services	1	9.7	8.2	81.1
	IFC Advisory Services	0	21.9	18.8	59.4
Design appropriate to meet objectives	World Bank Knowledge Services	0	1	6.6	92.3
	IFC Advisory Services	0	6.3	12.5	81.3
Were there any relevant issues to the client the knowledge activity was not able to address?	World Bank Knowledge Services	6.1	67.3	14.8	11.2
	IFC Advisory Services	3.1	68.8	12.5	15.6

SOURCE: Independent Evaluation Group (IEG) knowledge activity reviews.
NOTE: NA = Not applicable. Some questions on the tasks (such as, Was the activity requested by the client?) were more objective than others (such as, Was the design appropriate to meet objectives?) and accordingly were less subject to observation errors. The indicators in the table average the responses across all tasks and are likely to average out the observation errors of responses on the individual knowledge activity.

Most often, Bank knowledge services were not able to address issues relevant to the client because reports provided very broad suggestions, with little operational or directional value (see also chapter 3, Technical Quality of Knowledge Services). This was the case for a report on private sector development in China produced in 2012 with focus on innovation systems. As the initial draft was very broad and did not meet client expectations, the final report was delivered with a one-year delay, after the publication of the 12th five-year plan, and could not inform it, as had been intended, in any meaningful way. In 2010, a broad comparative analysis of SME finance across Eastern European countries was conducted in the Russian Federation. Despite identifying major obstacles to SME financing, however, the report was short on specific measures that the authorities could consider implementing. In Kuwait, the Bank produced a report to support the National Strategy for Economic and

Social Development, but the design did not meet client expectations of an actionable plan to implement the "2010–35 vision" strategy previously elaborated by a global consulting firm. Instead, the report was seen as theoretical, with vague recommendations under each pillar and no specific "how to" guidance.

In some cases relevance was hampered by the lack of customized solutions aligned with client demand. For example, in Chile, the authorities were interested in strengthening the financial asset management system within the existing institutional framework, without a dramatic institutional change in the short term, but they were prepared to consider a substantial institutional change in the long term. The Bank's 2010 knowledge activity on financial asset management insisted from the beginning on drastic institutional change—creating a new independent financial management unit outside the Ministry of Finance—and never came to grips with providing a short-term operational solution. Sometimes the Bank's knowledge services, while relevant to the client overall, missed specific relevant issues that would have further increased its value. For example, in Bulgaria, the 2012 report on public expenditure for growth and competitiveness would have been of greater value to the client had it included an analysis of "nonprice competitiveness" to provide input for the authorities' discussions with the EU. In Thailand, the Bank's TA on tax incidence addressed relevant issues for counterparts but did not address tax incidence by industry, which the Tax Revenue Department would have wished to also assess. Overall, additional Bank effort should go into ensuring that clients' expectations from knowledge services are clearly understood so that the end products meet these expectations or appropriate follow-up work is done. In China, the IFC Advisory Services on leasing changed objectives over the life of the project; a programmatic approach would have been more appropriate, with front-end analytical work. The Sichuan Recovery Investment Program did not have flexibility in objectives and design to respond to rapid changes in priority or need given the emergency nature of the project. In South Africa, the design of support to the Women's Entrepreneurship Program did not consider financial sustainability and the program could not continue after IFC support stopped. Scalability was thus limited as the program covered fewer than 200 women and was not replicated.

In many cases, IFC Advisory Service projects are developed to demonstrate to clients the importance of issues or the feasibility of particular solutions, and they succeeded in doing so. In China, for example, the initial project on secured transactions was meant to raise awareness of the benefits of establishing a regime, leading to eventual government adoption of a modern system. In the Russian Federation, the initial work on reducing administrative barriers—a study and a dissemination strategy—was meant to get government buy-in to reforms, which were supported by IFC Advisory Services. However, work on competition in South Africa, which was not well received by counterparts, illustrates the risk of embarking on projects with weak client ownership.[4]

Use of World Bank Group Knowledge Services and Stakeholder Engagement

As the Bank Group responded to multiple demands in the focus countries, the knowledge services delivered have generally had multiple uses. Raising stakeholder awareness was the predominant use of Bank knowledge activities (figure 2.1). Use for other purposes—such as reforming government programs, helping reach consensus for change, building capacity, supporting to policy dialogue, informing new laws and regulations, and creating or improving institutions—was observed almost equally frequently, in about half of

FIGURE 2.1 Use of World Bank Knowledge Services and IFC Advisory Services (in % of Reviewed Activities)

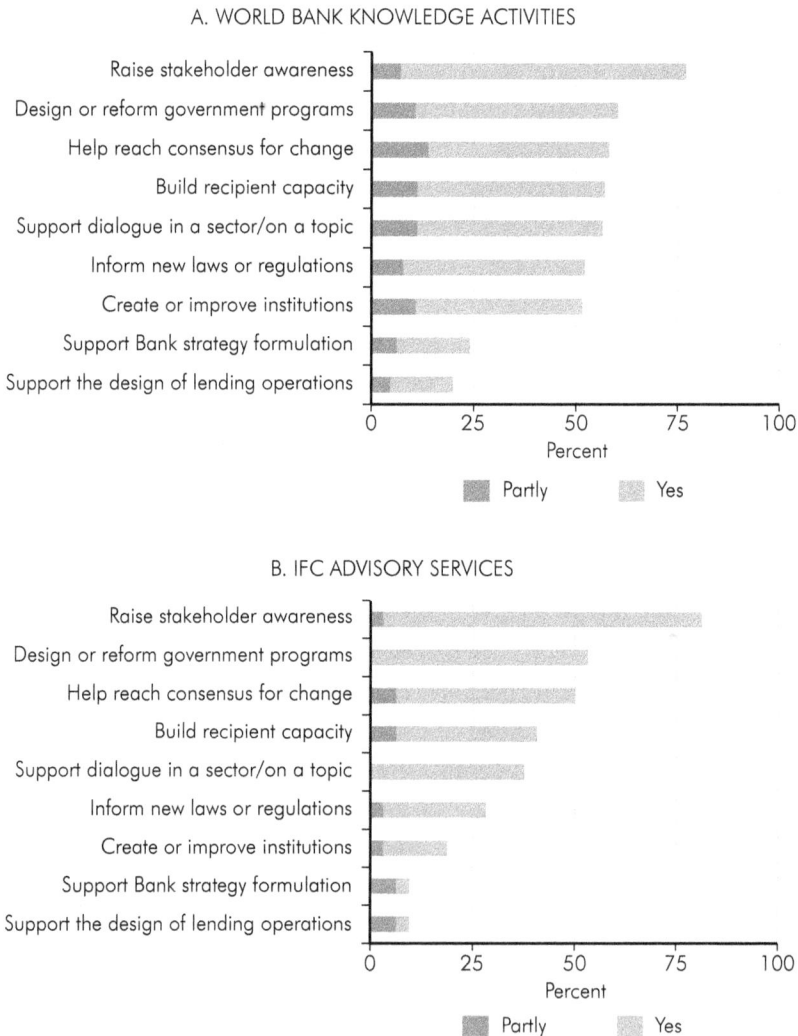

A. WORLD BANK KNOWLEDGE ACTIVITIES

B. IFC ADVISORY SERVICES

SOURCE: World Bank Group.

the knowledge activities reviewed. Support to Bank strategy formulation or to lending operations was a much less frequent use of knowledge—as expected in view of the overall limited lending in these countries. The overwhelming majority of IFC Advisory Service projects aimed to raise stakeholder awareness (figure 2.1b). This is crucial in projects that aim to introduce new practices, such as the use of credit bureaus, or influence the design of certain reforms, such as reducing the cost of real estate transactions or tax compliance costs for SME. Supporting policy dialogue and informing new laws and regulations were the next two major uses.

Client participation (full or partial) in the Bank Group's knowledge activities was generally high—an indication of client interest and relevance of the work conducted. Client participation was highest at the scoping stage of Bank knowledge activities and at the review and feedback stages, where it reached almost 80 percent of knowledge activities reviewed by IEG (figure 2.2). Participation was also high at the design and dissemination stages and relatively less frequent during implementation and analysis of results, reaching about 60 percent. Clients participated in the formulation of recommendations in almost half of the knowledge activities reviewed. Somewhat different from Bank knowledge activities, client participation in IFC Advisory Services was high not only at the design stage but also during implementation (figure 2.2). Discussions of Bank knowledge services with senior policy makers took place in the great majority of activities reviewed by IEG and somewhat less frequently for IFC Advisory Services (table 2.2).[5] The World Bank typically takes the lead in dialogue on policy issues, especially at the senior levels of government, with IFC working at the technical levels. This informal coordination of policy and technical dialogue between the Bank and IFC has worked fairly well in some cases reviewed by IEG in the focus countries—for example, in the work in the Russian Federation on reforming land transactions and subnational Doing Business environment or in the IFC financial sector work in China—but less well elsewhere, as, for example, the work on competition policy and administrative barriers in South Africa.

The frequency of full dissemination of Bank knowledge services was relatively low, conducted in slightly more than half of knowledge activities reviewed (table 2.2). In many cases the reports were disseminated internally and externally, with participation of civil society organizations, and served to promote a broader consensus on the reform agenda. A good example is the knowledge activity conducted in Bulgaria. The 2007 Country Economic Memorandum, with a strong focus on education, was disseminated in a session with Parliament, organized jointly with a think tank. The series of reports on regulatory reform were disseminated through public hearings organized by the Ministry of Economy, with participation of think tanks and professional associations. By contrast, broad dissemination has been a weak point of the Bank engagement in Kazakhstan, perhaps reflecting the

FIGURE 2.2 Participation of Government Counterparts in Knowledge Activities (in % of Reviewed Projects)

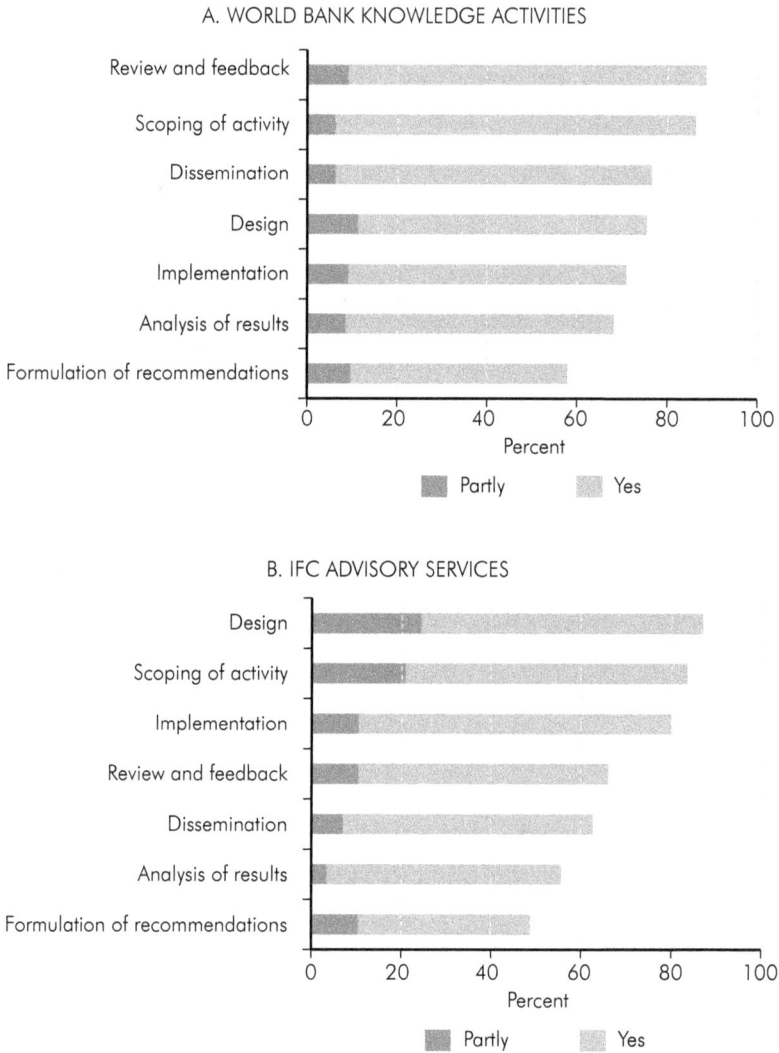

A. WORLD BANK KNOWLEDGE ACTIVITIES

B. IFC ADVISORY SERVICES

SOURCE: World Bank Group data.

authorities' preference. For example, as brainstorming sessions are confidential, lessons learned or a summary of the discussions are not disseminated to a wider audience, and little if any of the Bank's knowledge services is being discussed openly with representatives of business associations and other stakeholders. Full dissemination of IFC Advisory Services was more frequent than for Bank knowledge services. The confidentiality often imposed on Bank knowledge services cofinanced by clients or through RAS explains to a large extent the lower rate of dissemination of Bank knowledge services.

TABLE 2.2 Outreach of Bank Group Knowledge Services

Indicators	Categories	Percentage			
		NA	No	Partly	Yes
Product of the activity discussed with senior policy makers	World Bank knowledge services	3.6	4.6	7.7	82.7
	IFC Advisory Services	15.6	12.5	3.1	68.8
Product of the activity disseminated and covered by the media	World Bank knowledge services	2	29.6	11.2	55.6
	IFC Advisory Services	6.3	18.8	3.1	71.9

SOURCE: Independent Evaluation Group knowledge activity reviews.

NOTE: NA = Not applicable. Some questions on the tasks (such as, Was the activity requested by the client?) were more objective than others (such as, Was the design appropriate to meet objectives?) and accordingly were less subject to observation errors. The indicators in the table average the responses across all tasks and are likely to average out the observation errors of responses on the individual knowledge activity.

Strategic Positioning of the World Bank on Development Knowledge

IEG's review of the World Bank's role as a knowledge service provider in the focus countries broadly confirms that the Bank succeeded in strategically repositioning itself as a relevant development partner despite diminishing engagement through finance. Counterparts interviewed by IEG generally acknowledged four strengths in the Bank's knowledge services that enhance their relevance and help maintain the Bank's position as a knowledge partner of choice:

• Ability of benchmarking against international best practice through cross-country comparisons

• Reputation as an independent and credible broker of knowledge with a partnership approach

• Knowledge of the local context and capacity to customize international best practice solutions

• Capacity to see the big picture and analyze cross-sectoral issues important for development.

International benchmarking. In several countries, counterparts were most appreciative of knowledge activities based on standard methodologies developed by the Bank, providing a diagnosis and benchmarking against international best practice. This was the case in Kuwait with regard to the Country Procurement Assessment Review (CPAR), Public Expenditure and Financial Accountability (PEFA), and FSAP reports. The Russian Federation and Kazakhstan particularly appreciated knowledge services that enabled benchmarking of performance with peer country groups—including at the subnational level in the Russian Federation—with use of methodologies, such as ICAs and Doing Business, that were not easily replicable by other partners. Application of these methodologies is generally appreciated on important private sector development issues where there has not been systematic thinking, such as economic diversification, innovation, and competitiveness. Similarly, in Malaysia, the Bank is considered particularly well positioned on economic analysis and knowledge of international experience. Counterparts tend to turn to the Bank for cross-country comparisons, and to consulting firms (Boston Consulting Group, McKinsey) for Malaysia-specific issues.

Independence and credibility. This attribute of Bank knowledge services came often on top of counterpart views. Perceptions of independence and credibility of high-quality work helped the Bank to succeed in its re-engagement with Malaysia after more than a decade of absence. In Kuwait, counterparts see the World Bank, in comparison to other consulting firms, as an independent broker of knowledge, with high integrity, a partnership approach, high-quality standards, and the capacity to transfer best international practices and experiences. In Chile, an OECD member country, the Bank is still widely recognized as a credible and neutral partner that can be relied upon for good-quality advice. But in South Africa, the Bank has faced more challenging conditions in delivering a knowledge-based country program, due to the unique social political economy of this country. The views within the government on strategy and policies are diverse and reflect different political ideology of different interests. A common criticism has been that some recommendations did not take into account local context, as in the cases of IFC Advisory Service projects with the Department of Trade and Industry. Given the lack of consensus on policy directions, the Bank's attempt to engage on the policy dialogue as an independent and credible knowledge broker was marginally successful. However, the Bank is still well regarded and it has been relatively more successful in responding to demand-driven Advisory Service requests drawing on its extensive international experience. Perhaps surprisingly, some of the most appreciated Bank contributions in China were on topics of a controversial and politically-cum-institutionally sensitive nature, such as land policy reform, delivery of rural public services and their financing mechanisms, food safety, and the economic value of scarce water resources. At the same time, the government requested IFC help in improving product quality and corporate governance, and introducing corporate and social responsibility guidelines to private sector and state firms. As long as the Bank takes a holistic, fundamental, and nonconfrontational approach and uses evidence-based—as opposed to ideology-driven—analysis, counterparts in China felt that they were confident enough to handle tough messages.

Customization to local context. A distinct strength of Bank knowledge services mentioned by counterparts interviewed by IEG is the Bank's deep knowledge of the local context. As underlined, for example, by stakeholders in Kazakhstan, this knowledge is reinforced by the presence of the Regional Office for Central Asia in Almaty. IFC Advisory Service projects in the Russian Federation have used a combination of local working groups with international experts in formulating recommendations. In Thailand, unlike other development agencies, the Bank is seen by counterparts as having the capacity to properly customize international best practice to the Thai context because of its knowledge of local institutions that comes mainly from the expertise of staff in the Regional Country Office in Bangkok.

However, the Bank's recognized capacity to customize knowledge services to the local context might, to some extent, be challenged in the future by the lack of sufficient knowledge activities to gain appropriate depth and breadth of country knowledge. This is a risk mainly when the Bank works through RAS and does not maintain local presence. In Chile, for example, where the program is managed from the Regional Office in Peru, the Bank has not conducted a comprehensive assessment of development priorities since the 2006 Development Policy Review and does not conduct Public Expenditure Reviews or similar cross-cutting studies.[6] The Bank participated in an FSAP update led by the International Monetary Fund (IMF) in FY11. Country visits are being conducted occasionally, to gain perspective on macroeconomic developments and structural policy issues. However, it is questionable whether this is enough for the Bank to maintain a solid analytical base and policy expertise on the country. This might create a gap in the practical relevance of the Bank's knowledge services, as already seen in some cases. For example, work on the decentralization of education and health validated the authorities' views on the subject but lacked some practical aspects for implementation. Similarly, some of the work on improving public sector management was conceptually sound but did not refer enough to local Chilean processes to be of practical implementation value.

Capacity to see the big picture and deliver multisector development solutions. A strength of the Bank's knowledge services often emphasized by counterparts, as, for example, in the Russian Federation, was the ability to see the big picture and provide credible advice on the role of government versus the private sector on topics such as economic diversification and innovation. Global consulting firms are seen as quite good in providing narrow technical advice but have less credibility on policy matters. In China too, the Bank enjoys a special advantage in cross-sectoral activities. This advantage stems in part from the Bank's wide exposure to a variety of sectors, through lending or knowledge services, and in part from the government's difficulty to assign cross-sectoral mandates in China's administrative system. The ongoing road safety knowledge product illustrates this. Thanks to the Bank's expertise and project experience in the various areas—health, road design and services, and others—it brought together sectors that until now were disjointed from the point of view of road safety.

Again, this advantage might be challenged by the growing tendency of the Bank to deliver knowledge services through the "consultant firm model," with insufficient follow up and emphasis on important issues for the development agenda. This has been the trend of engagement, for example, in Chile where the Bank works certainly in a demand-driven orientation but sometimes in a piecemeal manner, with insufficient follow up and with insufficient emphasis over time on issues that have been identified as important for medium-term development. Examples include the work on innovation policy where the Bank's work was virtually suspended following the change in government priorities and the cancellation of the Innovation and Competitiveness investment loan. The programmatic TA on poverty and equality of opportunity was initially used as an input for discussion in the Presidential Council. However, contrary to plans, the work on assessing inequality of opportunity in Chile was discontinued because of the change of priorities of the new government. Moreover, the Bank's self-imposed boundaries of intervention often keep it out of debates on the long-term development agenda. For example, the Bank is not part of the debate on the all-important long-term issues of labor productivity, innovation, and climate change. Counterparts outside of the government miss the Bank's contributions and participation in these areas.

The Bank's main strengths in knowledge, as perceived by stakeholders in the focus countries, are intimately linked to the Bank's roles as "knowledge producer" and "knowledge customizer." They are also linked to its role as "knowledge connector," as the Bank's convening power was often used in the focus countries to mobilize top international experts for brainstorming sessions and seminars with high-level government officials (as, for example, in Kazakhstan and Malaysia), or for TA and working sessions with government agencies to address more specific issues (as, for example, seminars on transfer pricing or on anticorruption organized in Thailand).[7] The results of client surveys in four of the focus countries are broadly consistent with the analysis in this report, underscoring the importance of sharing knowledge about international best practices and of the technical quality of knowledge services (see box 2.2.)

There is room for further enhancing the Bank's relevance as knowledge connector by intermediating more efficiently the knowledge acquired in countries with knowledge-based programs. There were ample opportunities for learning from development experiences in the focus countries. For example, the engagement in Chile generates highly relevant knowledge for other countries in view of Chile's progress in several areas of public policy (education financing, program budgeting, pensions, insurance) and strong institutional capabilities (for example, on the evaluation of policy programs). Malaysia's development trajectory from low-income to upper-middle-income economy, and its central place in the Association of Southeast Asian nations (ASEAN) community, holds relevant knowledge for other countries.

The Bank systematically conducts Country Opinion Surveys in client countries to enhance understanding of how stakeholders perceive Bank work. Country Opinion Surveys are available for four of the focus countries: Bulgaria (FY12), Chile (FY10), China (FY12), and South Africa (FY12). A reading of the section on knowledge indicates that views expressed by stakeholders surveyed were broadly consistent with the analysis in this report.

- In Bulgaria, over half of the respondents indicated that the Bank's greatest value was its knowledge and advisory services. The greatest weakness respondents (23 percent) found was that there was not enough disclosure of the Bank's work, and that in some instances, the Bank tended to impose technocratic solutions without regard to political realities (22 percent). When asked how the Bank could be of greater value, more than 40 percent of respondents indicated that it should offer more innovative knowledge services.

- The greatest value perceived by respondents in Chile (52 percent) was the Bank's technical advice, and producing knowledge and research that are useful (44 percent). The ability to adapt its knowledge to a country's needs received a relatively lower rating than other ratings related to the Bank's knowledge services, and over half of respondents indicated that the Bank's greatest weakness was the little effort devoted to disseminate its analytical work and policy proposals. A number of respondents reported that the key way to increase the Bank's value was by adding more value to the internal policy debate through its international experience, and technical assistance.

- In China more than 40 percent of surveyed stakeholders felt that the greatest value provided by the Bank was the transfer of international best practices and new concepts and innovations. According to 30 percent of those surveyed, the greatest Bank weakness is that it fails to adapt global knowledge to local conditions. Nearly 40 percent of respondents indicated that in future the Bank—to be more valuable to China—should improve the quality of its experts as related to China's specific challenges, while 30 percent said the Bank should offer more innovative knowledge services.

- In South Africa—where there was a very low stakeholder response (14 percent) and which showed the lowest scores of the four client surveys—technical assistance was seen by respondents as an important value the Bank brought, although financial resources were seen as the item bringing the most value. The weaknesses identified by respondents were not enough public disclosure of Bank work, and Bank staff not being accessible enough. Respondents saw scope to improve value through more responsiveness and staff accessibility, and by having experts who are familiar with South Africa's specific development challenges. The low response rate may indicate that responses are not representative of the stakeholder sample.

SOURCE: Latest country surveys for Bulgaria, Chile, China, and South Africa.

Counterparts interviewed by IEG saw the Bank as a platform to share Malaysia's experiences with other developing countries. Malaysia has offered to host regional experience sharing events in the past (regional conference on investment climate), although evidence on the effectiveness of this activity was difficult to come by. In Kazakhstan, the findings and recommendations of some knowledge activities, such as study on oil funds and the sovereign wealth fund, could be useful to other countries. In Kuwait, the program generated knowledge, such as the analysis in policy notes on the governance and integrity program, which could be relevant to other countries in the Middle East and North Africa. As China—and other upper-middle-income countries—becomes an increasingly important provider of global development assistance, greater understanding of its successes and failures, especially with a global perspective, will help other countries assess the relevance of the Chinese model to their own development challenges. In particular, issues related to land and water scarcity—tenure security, registration and cadaster, productivity of land—are concerns worldwide, especially in the Middle East and North Africa and much of Sub-Saharan Africa, and the Bank could play a useful role in facilitating exchanges based on the knowledge acquired in China.

There are some good examples where the Bank's knowledge services facilitated South-South exchanges and policy dialogue in the focus countries (see chapter 4), but more can be done as the Bank's geographic, thematic, and organizational fragmentation prevents the full potential of such exchanges to be realized. In China, for example, while the World Bank Institute's technical assistance work has focused squarely on catalyzing lessons for other developing countries, it appears that the Bank has not fully exploited the potential of this mutual learning opportunity. The Russian Federation, for example, could benefit from the extensive work the Bank has done in China on regional approaches to investment promotion. Lessons from this experience have not been transmitted to the Russian Federation. Knowledge sharing is often hampered by the confidentiality of the work conducted through RAS. In Kuwait, there has been no transfer of knowledge to other countries given the confidentially of the studies. Intermediation of knowledge often takes place only informally, through Bank staff working also on other countries or through South-South exchanges initiated by clients and sometimes facilitated by the Bank. In Chile, the Bank has used mostly its informal networks, through the task team leaders and network management, to convey knowledge acquired in Chile to other countries in Latin America and elsewhere. In Kazakhstan, some government agencies have already shared their experiences with other countries in the region. For example, the Statistical Agency is sharing its experience with Azerbaijan and other countries in the region without World Bank intervention.

The strengths and weaknesses of the Bank's knowledge services in the focus countries determine, to a large extent, the way the Bank is perceived by clients in its positioning as a development partner with respect to other institutions—other international financial institutions, universities, think tanks, and global consulting firms. It should be noted that, in keeping with the Bank's mandate as an international development institution and its policy statements, "strategic positioning" is meant here to illustrate how the Bank is perceived *as a strategic partner and policy advisor*, not whether the Bank could position itself as a consultancy firm competing for advisory contracts, which is irrelevant to its mission.[8] Based on IEG interviews of stakeholders, the Bank's strategic positioning with respect to other knowledge providers is generally favorable, but varies across countries and thematic areas of work. The Bank's strategic positioning also depends on the mode of knowledge services financing as the presence of other knowledge service providers is more intense when the Bank's knowledge services are being delivered as a RAS than as a public good. A summary of the World Bank's perceived strategic positioning in the focus countries is in Appendix G.

The strategic positioning of IFC Advisory Services in focus countries is based on institutional or practice gaps (or market failure) in areas relevant to the CPS, and IFC uses the "additionality"[9] of Advisory Services to enable the implementation of reforms to address these gaps. There is intensive awareness-raising and dissemination of IFC work as well as piloting. Results are based on government action, irrespective of whether the subsequent TA is delivered by IFC or others. However, IFC does not have the resources to provide TA, for example, to all provinces in China or support all entrepreneurship programs in South Africa. In a sense, IFC opens up the market for others, in the same way that IFC investments are meant to encourage other private sector investments. IFC has a poverty focus, with emphasis on IDA and fragile states, and it would thus typically reallocate resources to poor countries if Advisory Services have no impact in upper-middle-income countries with World Bank knowledge-based programs. IFC continues to work in some larger middle-income countries—such as China and Russia—with an emphasis on public goods or frontier areas with a disproportionate lower-income population.

Overall, despite variation across countries and sectors, the Bank has succeeded in capitalizing on some key strengths (international experience, credibility and independence, customization, multisector expertise) so as to remain relevant and maintain a good strategic position in the countries where it engages mainly through knowledge-based programs. Risks that may erode these strengths in the future would merit attention. They reflect in particular the possible loss of breadth and depth in analytical knowledge of country clients, and the insufficient focus on medium-term country development challenges as a result of increasing concentration on RAS in high client demand. The Bank's overall relevance could be further enhanced by improving the way the Bank intermediates the knowledge acquired in country clients with knowledge-based programs.

Endnotes

[1] In 2010 the Bank elaborated an Interim Strategy Note for FY11–12, as a result of the 2008–09 global financial crisis that led to a resumption of lending to Thailand with a Development Policy Loan of $1 billion.

[2] The criteria are as follows: client need and ownership or market failure; intended development results; the distinct value IFC brings considering roles and activities by other stakeholders including other Bank Group institutions; strategic relevance, which includes fit with IFC and Bank Group strategies; links to other IFC projects; and risks.

[3] The Joint Economic Research Program (JERP) is a demand-driven, cofinanced program, whereby the government and the Bank annually agree on AAA to be conducted. The JERP grown from $1.3 million in 2004 (of which 40 percent was government financed) to $4.3 million in 2012 (of which 85 percent was government financed).

[4] The project was requested by the Competition Commission and Tribunal of South Africa, but the end-product was not to the liking of counterparts perhaps reflecting weak communications during project preparation as well as changes in counterparts who came with new priorities.

[5] Many IFC projects do not target policy makers, including, for example, programs supporting private sector entrepreneurship in South Africa, which mainly target private providers of programs and entrepreneurs.

[6] IEG is aware that in August 2012 the Bank appointed a liaison officer based in Chile to strengthen the dialogue on medium-term development issues in the country and monitor the program closely with the government.

[7] The Bank's three knowledge roles were analyzed in *"The State of World Bank Knowledge Services: Knowledge for Development 2011."*

[8] IEG understands that the Bank has never taken the policy position that it can or should act as a consultancy. In this report, the authors refer to the Bank sometimes becoming a de facto consultant to the government under a reimbursable knowledge service contract. For the definition of the Bank's role in the provision of reimbursable services. IEG acknowledges the inherent tension in remaining engaged with the development agenda while addressing the short-term priorities of clients under RAS. There are practical limits in a difficult budget environment for a business model that would require resources and generate no income, and the Bank could evaluate with clients essential strategic areas to be covered outside the RAS program.

[9] IFC additionality is the unique benefit or addition of value that IFC brings to a project, and that the client would not receive without IFC intervention.

3

Technical Quality of Knowledge Services

CHAPTER HIGHLIGHTS

- The majority of Bank knowledge services and International Finance Corporation (IFC) Advisory Services conveyed to the client international best practice and relevant examples, based on the Bank Group's global knowledge. Most tasks referred to the institutional and policy context and, to a somewhat lesser extent, generated some kind of new evidence and provided actionable recommendations.

- There was more variation in the degree to which the tasks used local expertise and discussed capacity requirements of recommendations.

- About 48 percent of Bank knowledge activities did not deploy, or only partly deployed, local expertise. Use of local expertise was more frequent in work on education and health, agriculture, and poverty and social protection.

- Actionable recommendations were formulated in 69 percent of Bank knowledge activities but their substance and attention to capacity requirements varied considerably across tasks.

- The capacity requirements and administrative feasibility of recommendations were discussed less frequently and were neglected in 25 percent of Bank knowledge services. They were addressed more frequently by activities in the financial sector and infrastructure.

This chapter reviews how the selected Bank Group knowledge services performed, as captured by three input factors: the transfer of global expertise, the customization of solutions to country context, and the development of actionable recommendations.

Leveraging the Bank's Global Expertise

It is, of course, difficult to compare the technical quality of heterogeneous knowledge services. But an indication of quality can be gathered from the knowledge inputs that went into the service. Inputs include deployment of global knowledge, consideration of the institutional and policy context, production of new evidence, development of recommendations, and consideration of capacity constraints for implementing recommendations. The great majority of Bank knowledge services and International Finance Corporation (IFC) Advisory Services conveyed to the client international best practice and relevant examples from the region or other regions, based on the Bank Group's global knowledge (table 3.1). A look at some examples covered in this study illustrates more specifically the myriad ways deployment of international experience can contribute to technical quality and to client use of the activity (for example, on regulations, programs, and capacity). Global knowledge can help benchmark existing institutions and policies, and guide reform toward best practices in these areas. In the focus countries, the Bank used very different knowledge vehicles, from broad-ranging reports to more narrowly focused advisory and custom-made technical assistance (TA), to convey global knowledge and international best practice. Successful tasks on the deployment of global knowledge ranged from broad to very specific applications.

TABLE 3.1 Transfer of Global Knowledge in Knowledge Activities and Advisory Services Reviewed by IEG

Indicators	Categories	Percentage			
		NA	No	Partly	Yes
Transfer of international best practice and relevant examples	World Bank Knowledge Services	2.6	4.6	14.8	78.1
	IFC Advisory Services	15.6	0	21.9	62.5

SOURCE: IEG knowledge activity reviews.
NOTE: NA = Not applicable. Some questions on the tasks (such as, Was the activity requested by the client?) were more objective than others (such as, Was the design appropriate to meet objectives?) and accordingly were less subject to observation errors. The indicators in the table average the responses across all tasks and are likely to average out the observation errors of responses on the individual knowledge activity.

At the broadest level, an example of a successful task was the Collaboration Forum for a Stronger Thailand that brought together international experts in a wide range of development topics. It helped inform new government programs on a rice disaster insurance scheme, increase attention to debt sustainability (with follow-up staff training from the Bank on public debt management modeling techniques), and introduce new concepts on financing public services, including ways to use public-private partnerships. The Kazakhstan Growth and Competitiveness—Issues and Priorities in the areas of Macroeconomic, Industrial, Trade, and Institution Development Policies activity also tackled a broad set of issues, and provided many examples of best practices as well as practices to be avoided, and relevant policy examples from other oil-rich countries.[1]

Mostly, however, Bank knowledge products focused on specific issues in the multiple sectors that the Bank covers. In much of its knowledge work, the Bank provided advice developed in a largely custom-made fashion to address specific client needs. A particularly successful example was the support for education policy in Chile, which brought in institutional experience from a set of good performing educational systems relevant to Chile (see appendix H). The South Africa Rural Development and Land Reform Reimbursable Technical Assistance conveyed global knowledge in both of these areas through its international consultants as well as seminars and study tours; these likely contributed to the many uses of the task including, for example, suggestions for improving and simplifying the cadaster system. China Air Pollution Control brought in advanced country knowledge on management of fine particles; it helped achieve a consensus to address the matter and expand monitoring and control plans. A hospital autonomy report under the Thailand Health Nutrition and Population knowledge activity brought in lessons from elsewhere to inform Thailand's difficult policy dialogue on decentralization. The Chile Implementation of Risk-Based Supervision Model for Insurance Industry brought in experience from Canada that informed new laws and regulations. In the Kazakhstan Poverty Monitoring task, the team shared a number of good international practices on survey instruments, and a study tour under the task conveyed international experience in data collection and dissemination at the U.S. Census Bureau in Washington. Work on innovation management in the Russian Federation focused primarily on international practices to provide advice to the Russia Venture Company on options for network models in supporting innovation; the company used its output to decide on the best network model for innovation programs. The Kazakhstan Higher Education TA brought in best practices by supporting a study tour of leading universities in the world, and then holding a seminar to review what was learned on the study tour and discussing a revised plan for the new university the government envisaged, with feedback provided by the universities visited. The TA may have helped establish a more autonomous university and initiated efforts to benefit from an international advisory panel of experts.

A number of knowledge activities brought in global knowledge through more standardized techniques and methods that rank high in client appreciation (see chapter 2), including Reports on the Observance of Standards and Codes (ROSCs), Financial Sector Assessment Programs(FSAPs), and Investment Climate Assessments (ICAs). The China Report on the Observance of Standards and Codes, which brought experience from Hong Kong SAR, China; Malaysia; Singapore; and Thailand, helped raise awareness of the shortcomings in the accounting industry and the urgent need to produce more high-quality corporate accounts and auditors to enable preparation of credible financial statements. Similarly, the Bulgaria Corporate Governance TA, which included a ROSC, a number of seminars, and other IFC Advisory Services for strengthening the Sofia stock exchange and increasing the number of corporations, brought in useful international examples and joint seminars that helped Bulgarian firms increase awareness and develop capital market regulation. The Russian Federation FSAP Update followed a methodology in line with international best practice and included a detailed assessment of the International Organization of Securities Commission principles of regulation, stress testing of the system, and an assessment of Basel Core Principles. The Central Bank widely used it as a supporting source of information and reference that added weight to its reform proposals. The Thailand Investment Climate Assessment activities provided international benchmarking that raised awareness and interest in investment climate policies and encouraged further work. The Malaysia Productivity and Investment Climate Assessment Update also provided international benchmarking, but its impact on awareness was probably weak.

Several IFC Advisory Service projects focused on disseminating global best practices as part of awareness-raising initiatives to generate interest in and ownership of reforms that are yet to be defined. In China, IFC Advisory Services on housing finance, leasing, and personal bankruptcy legislations were meant to expose authorities to global practices. The Advisory Services on secured transactions had several components, the first of which included exposure of stakeholders to best practices. In work on credit bureaus, IFC arranged seminars that included leading global players, shared best practice regulatory guidelines from other countries that were translated into Chinese, and facilitated the participation of Chinese officials in the World Consumer Credit Reporting Conference. In the Russian Federation, the work on introducing legislation that would enable emergence of securitization transactions involved reviewing best practice legal environments, while the outputs of the Advisory Service project on primary mortgage included a mortgage lending manual and mortgage borrower consumer protection regulation based on international best practice.

In a number of cases, however, the Bank did not deploy the global knowledge the tasks would have warranted. The China Private Sector Development Program, which called for advice on innovation systems, is one example. Similarly, there is no record that the Kazakhstan's Public Administration Reform or its Insolvency Framework—A Preliminary Overview delivered the global knowledge expected of them. In a few other cases, global knowledge appeared to be less critical for the task at hand, although they were likely to provide opportunities to bring in international experience. Examples are the Russian Federation Agricultural Policy Monitoring TA activity, which financed donor coordination efforts by the Bank to curtail overlap and contradictory advice from donors, and the China IFC Advisory Services—Access to Finance, which focused on reviewing the domestic situation in China by establishing baseline information through a survey that would be performed periodically.[2]

Customization of Solutions to Country Context

Bringing in global knowledge that is relevant to a country, as in the Chile Primary and Secondary Education knowledge activity (see appendix H) and the other examples above, is an important step in customizing to the country's context. It involves choosing the right comparators and the global practices that are appropriate for the country context. Accordingly, customization begins with reference to the institutional and policy context in the country. Furthermore, it may need generation of new evidence or data that inform analysis and recommendations. And both of these may also benefit from involvement of local expertise that is familiar with country conditions and data.

Most tasks generated some information and, not surprisingly, virtually all tasks covered by this study considered the country's institutional and policy context in one way or another (table 3.2). In contrast, about 48 percent of Bank knowledge activities did not deploy (or only partly deployed) local expertise. This may reflect unavailability of such expertise in some countries or sectors, a constraint on quality in such cases. Use of local expertise was frequent in work on education and health, agriculture, and poverty and social protection (figure 3.1). It was rare in work on the financial sector, where perhaps unavailability of expertise may be more binding, but was also infrequent in work on economic policy and public sector governance. Among the evaluation's focus countries, local expertise was used more frequently in Bulgaria, China, and South Africa, and less frequently in Kazakhstan, Kuwait, and the Russian Federation (figure 3.1). A look at the substance in the tasks indicates that attention to country policies and institutions varied in depth. Use of information ranged from reliance on existing data to conducting surveys that produced fresh new data. And use of local expertise varied from little or none to close

Thailand's economics of AIDS report (see appendix H) provides a good example of coupling strong deployment of international experience with thorough consideration of the institutional and policy context, production of key information (first estimates of cost effectiveness of

TABLE 3.2 Customization to Local Context in Knowledge Activities and Advisory Services Reviewed by IEG

Indicators	Categories	Percentage			
		NA	No	Partly	Yes
Reference to the institutional and policy context in the country	World Bank Knowledge Activities	1.5	1.5	14.3	82.1
	IFC Advisory Services	12.5	6.3	6.3	75
Generated new evidence and data that inform policy making	World Bank Knowledge Activities	2	10.2	17.3	69.9
	IFC Advisory Services	28.1	6.3	9.4	56.3
Use of local expertise	World Bank Knowledge Activities	3.6	31.1	16.8	48
	IFC Advisory Services	6.3	28.1	12.5	53.1

SOURCE: IEG knowledge activity reviews.

NOTE: NA = Not applicable. Some questions on the tasks (such as, Was the activity requested by the client?) were more objective than others (such as, Was the design appropriate to meet objectives?) and accordingly were less subject to observation errors. The indicators in the table average the responses across all tasks and are likely to average out the observation errors of responses on the individual knowledge activity.

interventions) for decision making on HIV/AIDS policy, and reliance on local health expertise. The other examples that follow illustrate the wide range of variation in the extent to which tasks considered the country context, produced new information, and engaged local expertise.

The South Africa Private Sector Development Activities (Small, Micro, and Medium Enterprises) was fairly strong in the three areas. It considered the country context, including economic trends, the role of small and medium enterprises, and industrial policies. It conducted a micro-enterprise survey that used the same core questionnaire of an Investment Climate Assessment—which would provide consistency for benchmarking—and added questions on the incentives framework; the survey was implemented using local expertise. The result was a credible report that was a major input to the government micro, small, and medium enterprises strategy. The Bulgaria Railways Policy Note is an example of thorough coverage of country context, use of existing data, and moderate use of local expertise. It was substantiated by a technical report that covered industry structure, markets, and operational and financial performance, with reference to international benchmarks, compilation of data from several

FIGURE 3.1 Use of Local Expertise in World Bank Knowledge Activities (in % of Activities Reviewed by IEG)

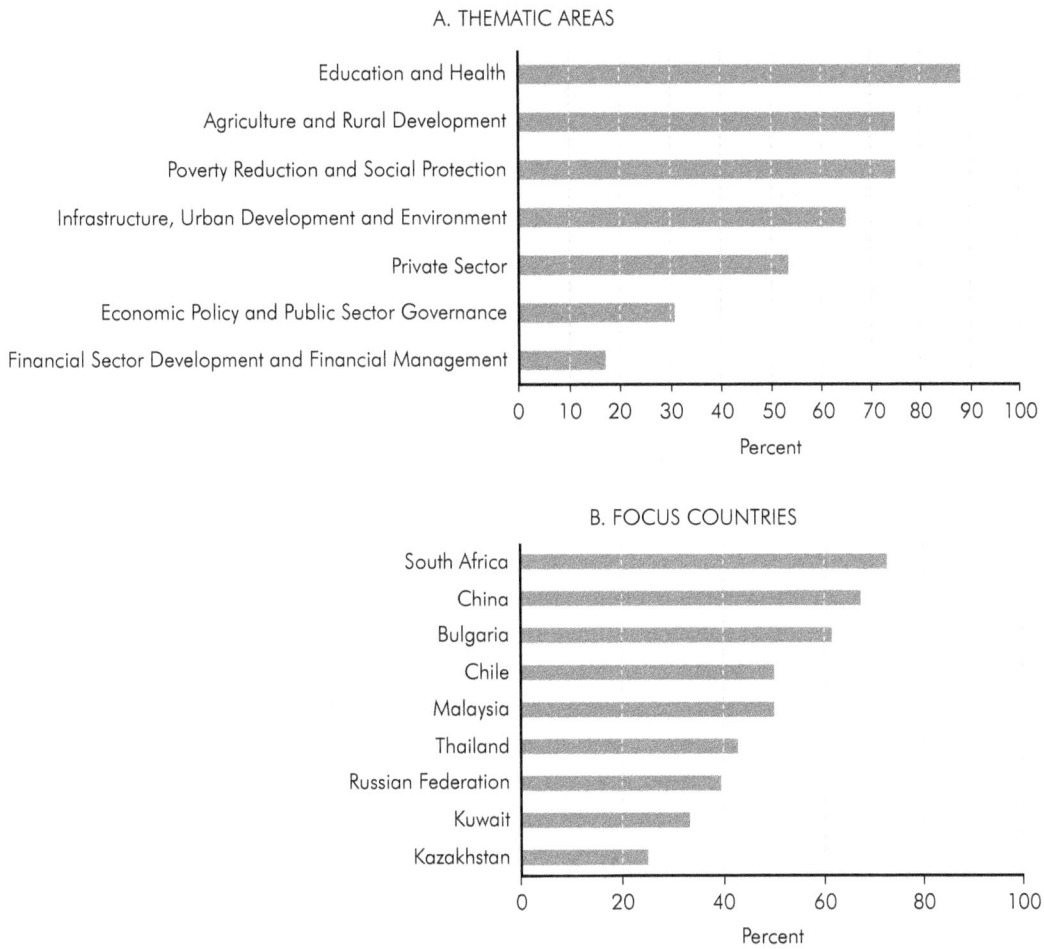

A. THEMATIC AREAS

Education and Health

Agriculture and Rural Development

Poverty Reduction and Social Protection

Infrastructure, Urban Development and Environment

Private Sector

Economic Policy and Public Sector Governance

Financial Sector Development and Financial Management

0   10   20   30   40   50   60   70   80   90   100

Percent

B. FOCUS COUNTRIES

South Africa

China

Bulgaria

Chile

Malaysia

Thailand

Russian Federation

Kuwait

Kazakhstan

0   20   40   60   80   100

Percent

SOURCE: World Bank data.

existing sources, and participation by counterparts in providing access to data and providing comments on drafts. In China, a capital market development project is an example of detailed coverage of the institutional and policy context and reliance on a local drafting team of experts to draft the report in Chinese, while using existing data. It contributed to capacity building at the Research Center of the China Securities Regulatory Commission and to raising the profile of commission and enhancing its role as the regulator of capital markets in China.

The China IFC Advisory Services on secured transactions and credit bureaus used programmatic approaches to expose stakeholders to best practices as part of the awareness-raising phase, followed by design discussion on how to blend best practices with local context, implementation of pilots to test customized solutions, and scaling up based on lessons from previous phases of the program. In the case of the Russian Federation, the IFC Advisory Services on securitization used a local working group and an international consultant providing inputs on international best practices, to ensure solutions that are feasible in light of the state of local institutions. The primary mortgage Advisory Services project also used a working group that brought together key market players to develop solutions that integrated best international practices and local context.

A number of reports were rather thin in the three areas of customization to country context. Outputs from the Russia Regional Development Strategy TA, including participation in international conferences, dissemination of the 2009 World Development Report, and a paper on intergovernmental relationships delved on country context and were used only to a very limited extent. A Chile Policy Assessment was likewise limited in its consideration of the country context and did not use local expertise or produce new data. There are no indications that it was used in any way by the government.

Development of Actionable Recommendations

A robust test of the quality or usefulness of a task is its ability to generate consistent and actionable recommendations with a foothold in the country's institutional reality and its capacity to implement the recommendations. Prioritization of recommendations will also contribute to the usefulness of knowledge activity outputs. Development of recommendations varied considerably across tasks in substance and in attention to capacity requirements. Actionable recommendations were formulated in 69 percent of Bank knowledge services. IFC Advisory Services were more often directed to demonstrate the feasibility of particular solutions to issues of interest to the client rather than formulating recommendations. The capacity requirements and administrative feasibility of these recommendations were discussed less frequently and were neglected in 25 percent of Bank knowledge services (table 3.3). Capacity requirements and administrative feasibility of recommendations was addressed more frequently by knowledge services in the financial sector and in infrastructure, and much less frequently by tasks in poverty and social protection and education and health. Among the focus countries, these institutional aspects of the recommendations were discussed more frequently by work conducted in China and Thailand and less frequently in Bulgaria, Chile, and the Russian Federation (figure 3.2).

The South Africa Sector Study of the Effective Tax Burden (described in appendix H) provides an example of a task with recommendations that were consistent with the analysis (in this case with the calculation of marginal effective tax rates), detailed enough to be actionable, and with a design that considered to some extent the administrative challenges of tax policy implementation. It recommended, for example, a declining-balance approach to depreciation

Indicators	Categories	Percentage			
		NA	No	Partly	Yes
Actionable recommendations formulated consistent with findings	World Bank Knowledge Services	3.1	6.6	20.9	69.4
	IFC Advisory Services	34.4	6.3	15.6	43.8
Analysis of capacity requirements and administrative feasibility of recommendations	World Bank Knowledge Services	6.6	25.5	25	42.9
	IFC Advisory Services	43.8	21.9	9.4	25

SOURCE: IEG knowledge activity reviews.
NOTE: NA = Not applicable. Some questions on the tasks (such as, Was the activity requested by the client?) were more objective than others (such as, Was the design appropriate to meet objectives?) and accordingly were less subject to observation errors. The indicators in the table average the responses across all tasks and are likely to average out the observation errors of responses on the individual knowledge activity.

allowances to improve administration and compliance. The other examples that follow below illustrate the wide variation across tasks in these dimensions.

The China Rural Public Services knowledge activity included a report aiming to improve the efficiency of capital expenditures with specific recommendations and attention to capacity that made them actionable.[3] Furthermore, the activity supported pilots to test the recommended institutional changes (for example, the use of block grants and performance-based grants) and the training programs to create institutional capacity. The Kuwait National Strategy for the Clean Development Mechanism Reimbursable Technical Assistance included a full report developing recommendations on institutional development. The task sought to provide advice on clean air investments and examined organizational options for the Designated National Authority to conform to the modalities and procedures of the Clean Development Mechanism, a credit scheme under the Kyoto Protocol to implement emission-reduction projects in developing countries. The TA considered five models based on international experience and settled on a single government department option. The recommendations spelled out the structure of the Designated National Authority (board, secretariat, and technical group) and the function of its units; the project approval procedures; and the sustainable development criteria to be met by projects, staffing, and capacity building needs. They clearly covered the "what" and the "how" that recommendations need to be of use. The Russia Programmatic

FIGURE 3.2 Discussion of Capacity Requirements and Administrative Feasibility of Recommendations in World Bank Knowledge Services (in % of Activities Reviewed by IEG)

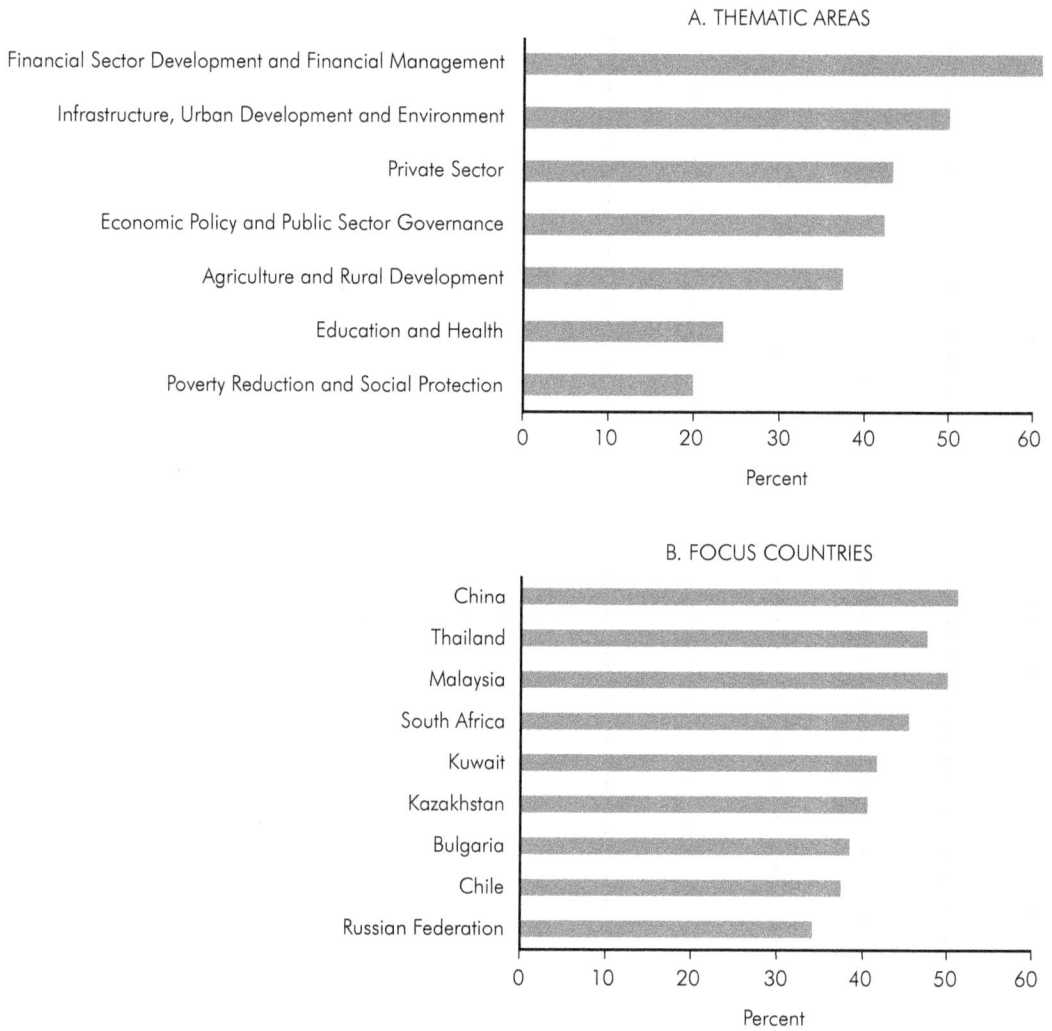

A. THEMATIC AREAS

Thematic Area	Percent
Financial Sector Development and Financial Management	~61
Infrastructure, Urban Development and Environment	~50
Private Sector	~43
Economic Policy and Public Sector Governance	~43
Agriculture and Rural Development	~37
Education and Health	~24
Poverty Reduction and Social Protection	~20

B. FOCUS COUNTRIES

Country	Percent
China	~51
Thailand	~48
Malaysia	~50
South Africa	~46
Kuwait	~42
Kazakhstan	~41
Bulgaria	~38
Chile	~37
Russian Federation	~34

SOURCE: World Bank data.

Poverty Work (Stage 2) developed specific recommendations to improve the targeting of social expenditures, consistent with its finding that only a small fraction of noncontributory resources was targeted to the poor and the few income-tested programs explicitly designed to serve poor or vulnerable populations had mediocre targeting.[4] Despite the well-considered recommendations, this knowledge service was not used. It is an example of a task with good overall technical quality, but that suffered from weak engagement of local stakeholders. The report *Accelerating Bulgaria's Convergence: The Challenge of Raising Productivity* provides a good example of attention to prioritizing recommendations by defining the top short-term and top medium-term reforms.

The recommendations developed in three of the knowledge services discussed above contributed to their use for different purposes. In contrast, a number of tasks suffered from weak attention to developing proposals and this contributed to their being used very little. A few examples will suffice. One is the South Africa Administrative Barriers IFC Advisory task, which did not flesh out its recommendations, with its quality also suffering from weak attention to country context. Similarly, in the South Africa Analysis of Investment Climate Variables, recommendations were general, bereft of implementation guidance, and with no discussion of capacity constraints or challenges. Neither of these studies was used to any significant extent.

 A few tasks were actually not designed to render recommendations. An example is the *Basel III Financial Architecture and Emerging Regulatory Developments in Macro Prudential Tools* (the Russian Federation), which did not have recommendations and aimed simply to create awareness of the changes in Basel III. It probably served to confirm the client's own conclusions and vision in relation to the impact of Basel III on the Russian banking system. Without recommendations, its use was commensurately limited.

Endnotes

[1] By way of examples, the report covered Chile's policy to successfully prevent real appreciation of the exchange rate and therefore protect competitiveness, the Republic of Korea's use conglomerates for development, the Kyrgyz Republic flat rate tariff policy, and China's use of the World Trade Organization to enhance domestic reforms.

[2] However, the IFC Access to Finance project was an important input to the issuance of a widely disseminated IFC paper "Promotion of SME: A Review of International Experience." Similarly, the two South Africa projects on small and medium enterprises (SME) tax burden and compliance costs focused on generating country information through surveys and not only international comparisons, practices, and experience; but the Advisory Services were part of larger effort in the Africa region that would enable comparison and analysis of different country practices.

[3] Key recommendations were: introducing lump sum ("block") grants to local governments with amounts that usually take into account spending needs, fiscal capacities, fiscal efforts of local governments, and other factors; basing rural project selection on a participatory planning and budgeting process, including participation in identifying and prioritizing local problems, finding solutions and preparing project proposals at the village level, and making final decision at the county level; developing monitoring and evaluation processes, instruments, systems, and funding; and reducing duplication among various funding programs by deriving projects from county-level comprehensive plans and allowing counties to use funds from other programs or sources for the counterpart funding requirement.

[4] The study submitted three options, with a detailed discussion of each: to strengthen the verification of household means, to replace the unverified income test with a proxy-means test, and to develop a hybrid means test.

4

Results and Their Sustainability

- Expected outcomes were achieved—or likely to be achieved—in 47 percent of Bank knowledge services and were partly achieved in another 37 percent. The frequency of outcome achievement was broadly comparable for Bank economic and sector work (ESW) and technical assistance.

- Outcomes of International Finance Corporation (IFC) Advisory Services were achieved in about 38 percent of projects reviewed.

- In general, knowledge service outcomes were more often achieved when the focus of the work was in relatively narrower thematic areas, rather than in broader themes, encompassing an ambitious reform agenda, or when the achievement of results would necessitate multisector efforts.

- The achievement of knowledge service outcomes was not correlated with financing arrangements for Bank knowledge services, probably owing to the high relevance of Bank knowledge services in countries with knowledge-based programs.

- Even though lending was limited, it remained a powerful driver of results for the Bank's knowledge services as at least partial achievement of expected outcomes of Bank knowledge services was observed more frequently when knowledge activities were used for the design of lending operations.

- Knowledge services with outcomes likely to be achieved more frequently had designs appropriate to meet their objectives, were requested by the client, and were able to address issues relevant to the client compared to knowledge services with outcomes unlikely to be achieved.

- Knowledge services that lagged in the achievement of outcomes were also weak in conveying international best practice, providing relevant examples, producing new evidence useful for policy making, formulating actionable recommendations, and discussing the capacity requirements and administrative feasibility of the recommendations.

- The lack of timely delivery of knowledge services to affect important decisions—not a prevalent problem in the sample of countries—was associated with poorer outcomes.

- Client participation in the various stages of knowledge services and participation of local experts were associated with the achievement of results.

- Knowledge services that achieved results have more often contributed to strengthening institutions and in building analytical and policy formulation capacity of recipients. This also contributed to the sustainability of these outcomes.

- Monitoring of Bank knowledge service results was weak for both individual activities and the country partnership strategy (CPS). Only 23 percent of knowledge activities included, at least partly, results indicators to track the achievement of the activity's outcomes. The majority of IFC Advisory Services were at least partly equipped with results indicators.

- Factors that influenced the degree to which World Bank and IFC knowledge services had synergy included the quality of the CPS results framework and the existence of core ESW. There is scope for improving coordination between World Bank and IFC, for example by including one institution in the other's review processes, especially at the concept and design stage.

This chapter first evaluates whether the expected outcomes of Bank Group knowledge services in the focus countries have been, or are likely to be, achieved. Next, it reviews the factors associated with the achievement of results of World Bank knowledge services. Third, it focuses on the sustainability of these results and the factors that may affect it. Finally, it reviews the synergy between World Bank knowledge services and International Finance Corporation (IFC) Advisory Services in promoting private and financial sector development in the focus countries.

Results of World Bank Group Knowledge Services

IEG's review reveals a mixed, though broadly positive picture for the achievement of results by knowledge services in the focus countries. Expected outcomes were achieved (or likely to be achieved) in 47 percent of Bank knowledge services (table 4.1). They were partly achieved in another 37 percent of knowledge activities reviewed. The frequency of outcome achievement was broadly comparable for Bank economic and sector work (ESW) and technical assistance (TA). Outcomes of IFC's Advisory Services were achieved in about 38 percent of the reviewed projects, lower than for World Bank knowledge services, while the frequency of projects that did not achieve their objectives surpassed that of Bank knowledge products. A first caveat applies to this assessment as the expected outcomes of Bank knowledge services are often not explicitly described and, even less, quantified in formal documents. Thus, expected outcomes often had to be inferred from the activities' design and overall stated purposes as well as from interviews with stakeholders and staff. A second caveat is that the results of knowledge services may potentially require a long time before they materialize, as the gestation period of

TABLE 4.1 Achievement of Expected Outcomes of Bank Group Knowledge Services (in % of Activities Reviewed by IEG)

Categories	Number of activities reviewed	Expected outcome of knowledge activity likely to be achieved		
		No	Partly	Yes
World Bank Knowledge Services	196	12.8	36.7	47.4
Of which, ESW	117	10.3	40.2	47.0
TA	79	16.5	31.7	48.1
IFC Advisory Services	32	21.9	25	37.5

SOURCE: IEG knowledge activity reviews.
NOTE: ESW = economic and sector work; TA = technical assistance.

difficult reforms may be long and capacity building or institution strengthening typically require significant time. Moreover, the Bank's knowledge services are often used to raise awareness or inform internal government debates, with the results appearing with substantial time lags. The Independent Evaluation Group's (IEG's) assessment of the achievement of knowledge service outcomes in the focus countries is thus surrounded by a degree of uncertainty as the observed achievement may be subject to change over time.

The assessment of outcomes for a task or group of tasks indicates the extent of progress achieved toward outcomes, including progress through the policy-making process. The assessment was based on the feedback obtained during the country visits and desk reviews and was limited by the generally weak monitoring of Bank knowledge activity results. The assessed progress varied from tasks that had little or no impact on policies (such as Investment Climate Assessments [ICAs] in Thailand), to tasks with recommendations that were being implemented, but with no visible impact on development outcomes thus far (for example, a report on student loans in Chile), and to tasks where development outcomes were already in evidence (for example, a report on inequality in China, see [Box 4.2]).

With these caveats in mind, the achievement of outcomes of World Bank knowledge services in the focus countries can be compared to the average performance ratings of World Bank lending operations to get some perspective on the relative success of the Bank's knowledge services when they are delivered as freestanding products. Over FY06–11, 74 percent of completed World Bank investment lending operations evaluated by IEG and about 82 percent of Development Policy Operations evaluated had a moderately satisfactory or higher development outcome rating.[1] On the other hand, the expected outcomes of about 84 percent of Bank knowledge services reviewed by IEG in the focus countries were likely to be *at least partly* achieved. Achievement of outcomes of Bank knowledge services in these countries—that make only limited use of Bank financing—thus slightly exceeded the average performance rating of Bank lending operations across regions. In the case of IFC, 58 percent of Advisory Services projects that were completed in FY08–10 and evaluated by IEG had ratings of mostly successful and higher ratings for development effectiveness. Using the (at least partial) achievement of expected outcomes as a proxy for overall development effectiveness, IFC Advisory Services projects reviewed in the focus countries with World Bank knowledge-based programs slightly surpassed overall IFC Advisory Services performance.

The degree of achievement of knowledge service outcomes varies across thematic areas of knowledge work and countries. Achievement (at least partial) of outcomes was higher than average in agriculture and rural development, education and health, and the financial sector. It was about average in infrastructure, urban development and environment, and lower than average in private sector development and in economic policy and public sector governance

(Figure 4.1). In general, knowledge activity outcomes were more often achieved when the focus of the work was in relatively narrower thematic areas, such as education and health, the financial sector, and subsectors in infrastructure. In broader thematic areas, calling for policy action or reform across several sectors, such as private sector development, economic policy, and public sector governance, expected outcomes were achieved less often. A caveat applies to knowledge service outcomes in these broader thematic areas, as the coordination of reforms across sectors may require more time to bear fruit, beyond the period covered by this evaluation. Outcomes were also different across the evaluation's focus countries. They

FIGURE 4.1 Achievement of Expected Outcomes of World Bank Knowledge Services by Thematic Area and Focus Countries (in % of Activities Reviewed by IEG)

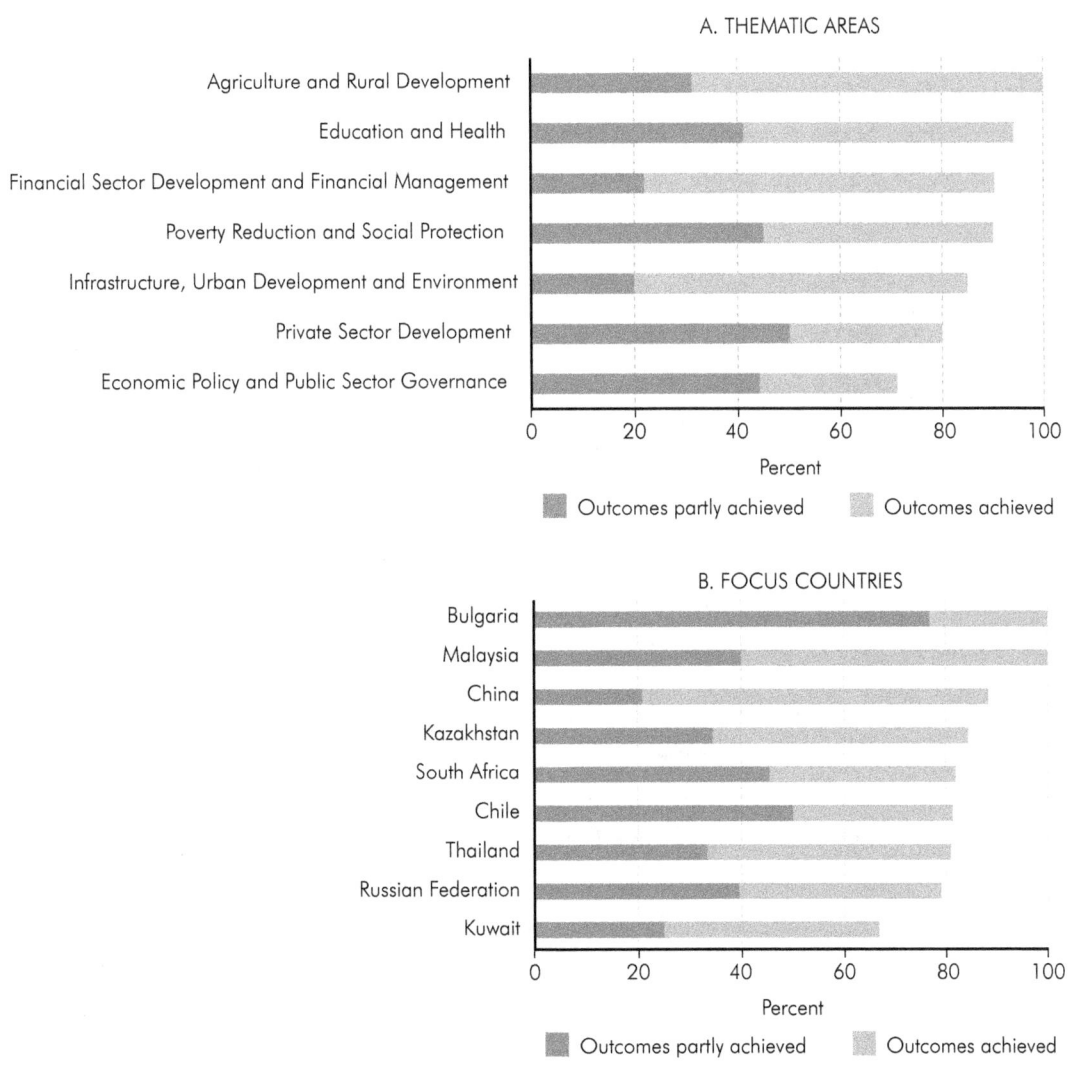

A. THEMATIC AREAS

B. FOCUS COUNTRIES

were at least partly achieved with higher frequency in Bulgaria, China, and Malaysia, and less so in Kuwait (Figure 4.1). A summary of results achieved in each of the focus countries of the evaluation is in Appendix I.

Achievement of outcomes of knowledge activities in poverty reduction and social protection was close to the average across thematic areas, although knowledge activities with partial outcome achievement were relatively frequent (figure 4.1). Despite the strides made by upper-middle countries in lifting millions out of poverty, these countries still face challenges in ensuring the sustainability of poverty reduction and protecting the vulnerable in the face of global economic swings. The Bank continues to be seen as a unique repository of knowledge in poverty reduction and social protection with knowledge activities conducted in almost all of the focus countries of the evaluation but will need to pay focused attention on the factors affecting the results of knowledge services in this area (box 4.1).

There are several examples of knowledge activities that have achieved results in the focus countries. Some of these activities generated information necessary for decision making, made a decisive contribution in raising stakeholder awareness, or contributed to strengthening counterpart technical capacity. For example, in China there is evidence that the recommendations of the report *Reducing Inequality for Shared Growth in China: Strategy and Policy Options for Guangdong Province,* a high-profile study conducted jointly with the provincial authorities, are being gradually implemented with concrete results in declining inequality (box 4.2). *The Economics of Effective AIDS Treatment* report in Thailand has been useful in providing the needed cost-benefit information to the government to increase the financing of antiretroviral treatment for AIDS patients, while the *Harm Reduction Policies and Interventions for Injection Drug Users in Thailand* report contains recommendations that are being implemented by nongovernmental organizations, in their HIV harm reduction programs. In education, although the recommendations of the recent skills report in Thailand are considered too general, skill-building is now a top reform priority for the government.

In Chile, the Bank's knowledge activity on higher education, conducted jointly with the Organisation for Economic Co-operation and Development (OECD), included a nationwide review and a review specific to the Bío Bío region. These have served as a shared reference for all stakeholders for ongoing reform efforts, while the Bank's work on student loans provided background for recent changes in policies. Another example of evidence-based knowledge services that led to results was the Water Quality Monitoring TA in the Russian Federation: techniques were tested in the Iset River Basin in parallel with preparation of a major revision to the Russian Federation's Federal Water Law. The knowledge generated from the Iset River Basin was subsequently transferred to assessments and mitigation efforts in 10

Social protection and poverty reduction knowledge activities accounted for about 9 percent of the activities reviewed. Those activities were recorded in seven of the nine countries covered (no Bank knowledge service in social protection or poverty reduction was done in Kuwait or South Africa during the period 2005–2012). Of 20 activities, including programmatic ones, six included technical assistance, either as freestanding interventions (three) or combined with economic and sector work. Thematically, interventions most frequently dealt with employment and labor market issues. Poverty monitoring and old-age security were also prominent, while safety net interventions were few. This may indicate that basic safety net structures are in place, albeit not always well funded, and that the focus has shifted to creating economic opportunity.

Stylized findings from the assessment indicate that the focus of the Bank's knowledge services in social protection and poverty reduction was on supporting the in-country policy dialogue and on providing solutions to specific policy issues as they arose. Over 80 percent of knowledge products fit into this category. Knowledge services did not feature prominently as a springboard for developing Bank strategy or for lending; such was the case in less than 25 percent of activities. In line with the focus on in-country policies, a large share of activities were either wholly initiated by the client or initiated in collaboration with the client; only 15 percent of activities were fully supply-driven. The activities drew heavily on local expertise; this was the case in some 75 percent of cases, largely above the average of knowledge services reviewed, while client participation in various stages of knowledge services ranged from 65 percent to 75 percent.

Results frameworks that would have allowed rigorous measurement of outcomes were absent in most instances. Still, all activities were completed, their recommendations discussed with policy makers in 85 percent of cases, and workshops were held, also in 85 percent of cases. Activities were mainly demand-driven, and local expertise, often from government or quasi-government institutions, were involved in most activities. These factors make it likely that the activities did influence policy making and policy design in a sustainable way. The assessment estimated that 80 percent of activities were likely to have at least partly achieved their expected results.

other river basins, including the Amur, Don, Koma, Neva, Ob, Ural, and Volga Basins. In Kazakhstan, the Bank's knowledge activities have contributed to building technical capacity in social protection (by providing, for example, Pension Reform Options Simulation Toolkit training for pensions) and led to policy changes. The introduction of a basic pension and consolidation of pension accounts were implemented as result of Bank recommendations.

BOX 4.2 Helping China's Guangdong Province Tackle Rising Inequality

Rising inequality in Guangdong, China's fastest growing and wealthiest province, is a challenge in view of the government's goal of achieving a harmonious society. Having decided to tackle head-on the challenge of rising inequality, the provincial authorities requested advice from the World Bank at a high-level meeting of the Bank Group's President and the Party Secretary of the Guangdong province at the end of 2007. The report, completed in 2009, was prepared jointly with a team of local experts, financed by the provincial authorities. It generated data and conducted analysis on poverty and inequality that provided new perspectives to the Guangdong authorities on the challenge of shared growth. Particular attention was drawn to the administrative requirements and governance aspects of measures that were suggested. However, the report could have paid more attention to the issue of intergovernmental fiscal relations, as transfers from the provincial government to local administrations and from the central government to the provincial government are essential for the sustainability of social safety net programs.

While it may be premature to assess the outcomes of this analytical work, so far the diagnosis and recommendations of the report have had a positive impact and are seen by the Guangdong authorities as valuable policy guidance. Counterparts highlighted that Bank recommendations are being implemented gradually, with focus on priority areas, including strengthening of public services and basic health care services, as suggested in the Bank report. In particular, in line with the recommendations of the report, the poverty line was increased from 1,500 Renmibi to 2,500 Renminbi. In December 2009 the provincial government launched a program of "Equalization of Basic Public Services in Guangdong," committing 2.5 trillion Renminbi to eight basic public services between 2010 and 2020, with the aim of leveling off differences in service quality and access in urban and rural areas. In health care, 96 percent of the population has been enrolled in the medical insurance scheme while investments were made in the construction of hospitals and health centers and in the training of health staff to better respond to the needs of the insured population.

There are indications that inequality in Guangdong has declined in recent years. Between 2008 and 2012, the proportion of urban to rural incomes in the province has declined from 2.96 to 2.67. In urban areas, over the same period, the ratio of the income of the highest and the lowest 20 percent percentiles of the population has declined from 6.8 to 5.3.

Where the Bank's advice was well-circumscribed, most often—but not exclusively—in the financial and infrastructure sectors, technical work helped achieve results. The Bank's Report on the Observance of Standards and Codes (ROSC) on accounting and audit standards in Kazakhstan provided the framework for the implementation of International

Financial Reporting Standards and International Accounting Standards, which has been successfully achieved for all large companies and financial institutions. Similarly, in Chile, following up on the Financial Sector Assessment Program (FSAP) recommendations, with support from the Financial Sector Reform and Strengthening (FIRST) initiative, all listed companies have switched to the International Financial Reporting Standards, while progress toward risk-based supervision in the non-banking sector has been significant. In the Russian Federation, the TA on the concession via public-private partnerships of facilities in Pulkovo airport, St. Petersburg, was highly successful, as it led to a contract with a group of investors and facilitated synergy with IFC through an investment for improving and managing those facilities. In Kuwait, although expected results have yet to materialize for most knowledge activities, TA to help the authorities articulate a strategy for emissions abatement was successful in positioning Kuwait as an applicant qualified to obtain Certificates of Emission Reduction under the Clean Development Mechanism of the Kyoto Protocol. In Thailand, the TA on risk-based tax audits has helped the Tax Revenue Department to develop new criteria for taxpayer classification that have already produced results in shortening the value-added tax refund time for big exporters. Similarly, the TA on procurement contributed to a better understanding of the scope of e-auctions and to the process of establishing a centralized procurement unit.

Results from knowledge activities have been partial in several cases, especially when the thematic area of the Bank's advice was broad in scope, encompassing an ambitious reform agenda, or when the achievement of results would necessitate multisector efforts. For example, in Bulgaria, results have been partial in education where progress in vocational and higher education is lagging, while in general education achievements have been concentrated in financing and school management, with education quality and student performance still lagging by international comparison. Similarly, while the regulatory framework of labor markets has been rationalized in line with advice by the Bank, skills gaps are prevalent and labor force participation remains weak. In Kazakhstan, the rationalization of higher education institutions was carried out, but not through the establishment of a quality assurance system, which was the key recommendation of the *World Bank/OECD Reviews of National Policies for Education* report.[2] In Thailand, the Bank's review of tax policy was used as an input to the government's 2011 tax reform, although only a limited number of recommendations have been so far implemented—such as, for example, reducing the corporate income tax but with no meaningful revision of holidays from the tax.

Although lending was not at the core of the partnership in the evaluation's focus countries, it remained a powerful driver of results for the Bank's knowledge services. The review reveals that at least partial achievement of expected outcomes of Bank knowledge activities was

FIGURE 4.2 Achievement of Expected Outcomes of World Bank Knowledge Activities (in % of Reviewed Projects)

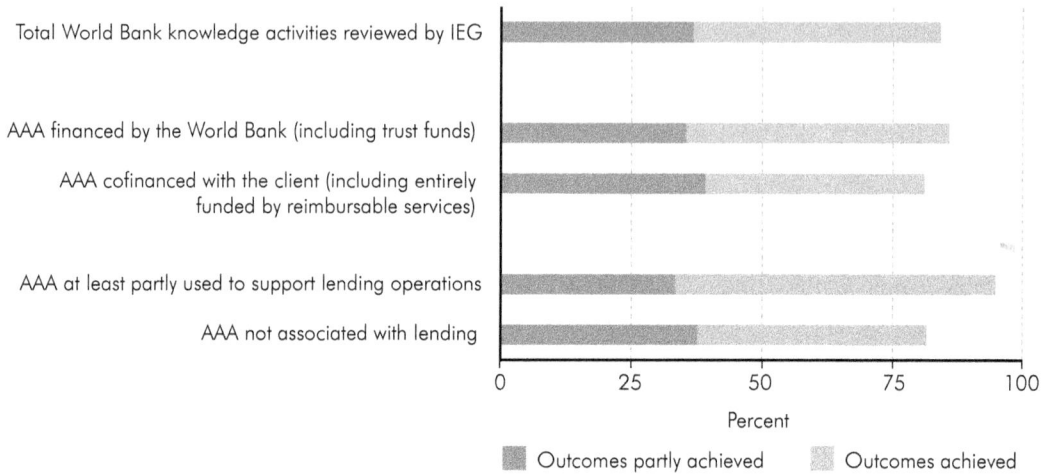

SOURCE: World Bank.
NOTE: AAA = analytical and advisory activities.

observed more frequently when activities were used for the design of lending operations. As borrowing in the focus countries is relatively limited, only 39 out of the 196 knowledge activities reviewed were used at least partly in support of the preparation of lending operations. In 95 percent of these knowledge activities, the expected outcomes at inception were likely to be at least partly achieved, against 81 percent in the case of knowledge activities not associated with lending operations (figure 4.2).

By contrast, the achievement of outcomes was not correlated with financing arrangements for Bank knowledge services. Among the 196 knowledge activities reviewed, 127 activities were financed by the Bank's budget (including trust funds) and 69 were cofinanced by the client (including 100 percent RAS). While outcomes were at least partly achieved in about 86 percent of Bank-financed knowledge services, this proportion was slightly lower, at 81 percent, in the case of knowledge services cofinanced or entirely financed by the client (figure 4.2). Reimbursable knowledge services are in principle expected to achieve better results as they are demand-driven and should benefit from stronger client focus and perhaps also stronger Bank effort. The absence of significant correlation between achievement of results and the mode of knowledge service financing reflects perhaps the high relevance to the client of Bank knowledge services in the focus countries with knowledge-based country programs, regardless of the financing arrangements underpinning the Bank's knowledge work. As noted in chapter 2, the majority of Bank knowledge services in these countries were demand-driven, as 81 percent of knowledge services was requested by the client, while client participation was very high in several stages of knowledge service preparation. When relevance and client participation are high, the mode of knowledge service financing appears to be less critical for the achievement of results.

IFC projects had mixed results. In China, IFC achieved results by using a programmatic approach to developing a credit information system and secured transactions regime, with the initial project focusing on raising awareness and later projects supporting various stages of development and implementation. IFC also focused its efforts on supporting investment promotion in Sichuan province with several projects, helping the province become a major destination for foreign direct investment. In the Russian Federation, two projects on securitization did not produce expected outcomes as a result of the financial crisis, which delayed enabling legislative and regulatory reform. However, there is high-level interest in the work on the subnational Doing Business database, which policy makers view as a useful tool for measuring regional performance in improving the investment climate. In addition, the three projects on reforming real estate procedures are beginning to show results as regions begin to address administrative barriers to private investment. In South Africa, there were disagreements or lack of interest from counterparts in IFC's work on competition policies and administrative barriers. However, projects on tax burden and compliance costs to micro, small, and medium enterprises (MSME) resulted in significant changes in tax policies. A project on credit information for microfinance was also successful, and there are plans to scale up the model to other segments of the financial system.

Factors Associated with the Achievement of Results of World Bank Knowledge Services

What factors are behind the achievement of outcomes of Bank knowledge services in countries with knowledge-based country programs? IEG's review focused on Bank knowledge services as the sample is large enough (196 activities) to permit robust analysis according to the degree of outcome achievement. The sample of IFC Advisory Services reviewed, consisting of only 32 projects, is too limited to allow robust analysis. Bank knowledge activities reviewed by IEG were classified according to the achievement of their expected outcomes (as portrayed in table 4.1): activities with outcomes expected to be fully achieved, activities with outcomes partly achieved, and activities where expected outcomes were not achieved.

The expectation underpinning the approach taken in this report (see chapter 1) was that relevance (objectives and design) and quality (global expertise, customization, and actionable recommendations) will surface as key factors for the outcomes. Quality and relevance to the client indeed appear to matter for the achievement of expected outcomes (table 4.2): Activities with outcomes likely to be achieved more frequently had designs appropriate to meet their objectives and were requested by the client compared to knowledge activities with outcomes

TABLE 4.2 Degree of Achievement of Knowledge Services Expected Outcomes in Relation to Knowledge Service Characteristics Evaluated by IEG (in % of Knowledge Services in Each Category of Outcome Achievement)

Indicators	Expected outcome of AAA likely to be achieved		
	Yes	Partly	No
Design of knowledge activity appropriate to meet its objectives	100	88.9	76
Activity requested or commissioned by client	87.1	80.6	72
Activity was unable or partly unable to address some issues relevant to the client	17.3	32	40
Activity conveyed international best practice and relevant examples	87.1	73.8	52
No new evidence or data generated to inform decision making	5.4	10	28
Local expertise used by activity	54.8	50	28
Actionable recommendations consistent with findings were provided	72	73.6	52
Capacity requirements and administrative feasibility of recommendations at least partly discussed	54.8	68	52
Activity outputs not delivered in time to inform important decisions	1.1	6.9	28
Activity disseminated and covered by media	65.6	52.8	36
Activity contributed to developing or strengthening institutions	51.6	31.9	16
Activity contributed to strengthening analytical or policy formulation capacity of recipient	71	45.8	20

SOURCE: IEG knowledge activity reviews.

NOTE: AAA = analytical and advisory activities. Some questions on the tasks (such as, Was the activity requested by the client?) were more objective than others (such as, Was the design appropriate to meet objectives?) and accordingly were less subject to observation errors. The indicators in the table average the responses across all tasks and are likely to average out the observation errors of responses on the individual knowledge activity.

FIGURE 4.3 Client Participation in Knowledge Activity Stages in Relation to Degree of Achievement of Knowledge Activity Expected Outcomes (in % of Reviewed Knowledge Activities in Each Category of Outcome Achievement)

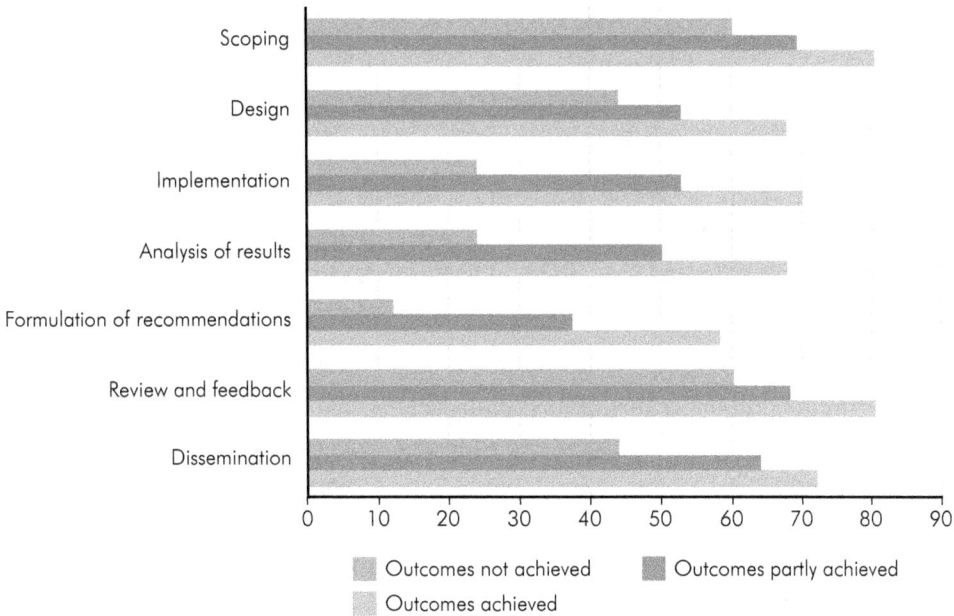

SOURCE: IEG knowledge activity reviews.

partly achieved or not achieved. Furthermore, activities with outcomes not achieved more often were unable to address relevant issues to the client compared to knowledge services with outcomes likely to be achieved. Activities lagging in the achievement of outcomes were also weak in conveying international best practice, providing relevant examples, producing new evidence and data useful for policy making, formulating actionable recommendations, and discussing the capacity requirements and administrative feasibility of the implementation of recommendations. Moreover, lack of timely delivery of knowledge services to affect important decisions appears to be associated with the failure to achieve the expected outcomes. There are abundant examples of knowledge services that achieved results and met very high standards of relevance and quality, but there are also counter examples of failure to achieve these standards and that confirm the rule that quality matters for results and highlight practices that need more focused attention by staff and management (see chapter 3).

IEG's review reveals that client participation in the various stages of knowledge activities was an important factor associated with the achievement of results (figure 4.3). In 60 to 80 percent of knowledge services where expected outcomes were achieved, client participation was noted in all stages of the activities. When knowledge service outcomes were partly achieved, client participation was observed less frequently, depending on the stage of the activity. Client participation was even less frequent when results were not achieved. When results were achieved, client participation was comparatively greater in the stages of implementation, analysis of results, and formulation of the recommendations. Building client ownership of knowledge services thus appears to be a key factor of results, together with the participation of local experts. Interlocutors often mentioned that the use of local experts and counterpart participation help ensure that global best practices are modified to take into account local conditions, recommendations take into account capacity constraints, and findings and suggested actions have ownership by stakeholders. In Malaysia, for example, client ownership of knowledge services delivered through fee-based services was strong and a local team was put together, including technical and steering committees, to work with the Bank. However, the knowledge activity, according to some, did not ensure appropriate depth and breadth of country knowledge as the work was still primarily done by international consultants. More engagement of local experts in tasks beyond support functions, such as collecting data, could have improved the relevance of the analysis (by providing, for example, more historical perspective of the phenomenon of brain drain) and the feasibility of the recommendations (for example, in the knowledge economy activity); and could have strengthened knowledge transfers (for example, in the modeling techniques used in the value chain analysis).

Bank-facilitated brainstorming sessions and seminars with high-level government officials are knowledge activities with strong client participation. They have been organized regularly in Kazakhstan, as a cornerstone of the Joint Economic Research Program, and they have also been organized in Malaysia. Brainstorming sessions in Kazakhstan appear to have been optimized by bringing together panels of high-level experts, providing clear policy messages based on international experience and customized to Kazakhstan. Although no formal framework to track results is in place, the brainstorming sessions appear to have had impact on issues such as resuming preschool education services, elaborating an anti-crisis package, establishing per capita financing in the health system, and providing impetus to an urbanization program. However, while brainstorming sessions are valuable for dialogue and can be highly influential on policies, they risk becoming a confidential exercise where the Bank's advice may lack impact because of political economy considerations, vested interests, or insufficient engagement of a broader set of stakeholders.[3] Options to mitigate this risk would include organizing open sessions, involving more interested stakeholders depending on the various topics, and keeping minutes of the sessions that could be disclosed, in consultation with the authorities, after a specified time.

Although the small size of IFC Advisory Services reviewed makes a systematic analysis of factors associated with results less robust, several factors identified in IEG's reviews were critical to the achievement of outcomes of IFC Advisory Services projects: Client ownership, clear objectives, quality of design, and the quality of monitoring and evaluation (M&E) systems were prominent among these factors. Use of programmatic approaches and strong links with IFC investment projects were also important. Paradoxically, some Advisory Services projects that were launched in response to demand from certain agencies did not produce strong results, sometimes because these were one-off initiatives with poor sustainability prospects. The project on insurance contractual law in the Russian Federation and the support to Endeavour, an entrepreneurship program in South Africa, were responses to client demand, but are not likely to achieve their intended outcomes. Use of projects to raise awareness or support pilot activities was critical to securing ownership and demonstrating benefits. The initial Advisory Services on secured transactions was not a response to a client request, but was able to generate client ownership for the creation of modern regime, supported by subsequent Advisory Services projects. Quality of design was a major success factor in the small and medium enterprises (SME) Banking project in South Africa, which established a microfinance credit information system. The project involved participation of banks where IFC had investments to demonstrate the benefits of using credit bureaus. Inability to restructure Advisory Services projects in the face of changing context adversely affected outcomes, as in the case of the Sichuan Recovery Investment Promotion project where the needs of the client evolved, and the project objectives and outcomes needed to be modified but were not.

Sustainability and Monitoring of Results

Sustainability of results of Bank Group knowledge services was in line with their achievement of results. The outcomes of 75 percent of Bank knowledge services and IFC Advisory Services reviewed by IEG were likely to be at least partly sustained (table 4.3). A majority of Bank knowledge services and IFC Advisory Services were complemented by other Bank Group activities, which may have contributed to the sustainability of outcomes. IEG's review reveals that 60 percent of Bank knowledge services contributed at least partly to developing or strengthening institutions. Similarly, a large majority of Bank knowledge services and a significant part of IFC Advisory Services contributed to strengthening analytical or policy formulation capacity of recipients. Institution building and capacity development raise the likelihood of sustainable results. Monitoring of capacity development objectives was, however, weak, especially for Bank knowledge services and less so for IFC Advisory Services. Capacity development outcomes in Bank knowledge services, when applicable, were at least partly monitored only in one-third of knowledge services reviewed by IEG. Furthermore, they were at least partly monitored in more than two-thirds of IFC Advisory Services reviewed.

The factors analyzed above, associated with the achievement of knowledge service outcomes, were also correlated with the sustainability of the outcomes (table 4.4). In the majority of

TABLE 4.3 Sustainability of Results and Capacity Building Outcomes of Bank Group Knowledge Services

Indicators	Categories	Percentage			
		NA	No	Partly	Yes
Outcomes of activity likely to be sustained	World Bank Knowledge Activities	10.2	9.2	25.5	50
	IFC Advisory Services	6.3	15.6	18.8	56.3
Knowledge activity complemented by other Bank Group activities including lending	World Bank Knowledge Activities	2	38.3	11.2	48
	IFC Advisory Services	3.1	21.9	12.5	62.5
Activity contributed to developing or strengthening institutions	World Bank Knowledge Activities	10.7	27	22.4	38.3
	IFC Advisory Services	21.9	46.9	9.4	21.9
Activity contributed to strengthening analytical or policy formulation capacity of recipients	World Bank Knowledge Activities	4.1	17.3	25	53.1
	IFC Advisory Services	25	15.6	18.8	40.6
Achievement of agreed capacity development outcomes monitored, and lessons learned used	World Bank Knowledge Activities	39.8	39.3	13.3	7.1
	IFC Advisory Services	59.4	12.5	15.6	12.5

SOURCE: IEG knowledge activity reviews.

NOTE: NA= Not applicable. Some questions on the tasks (such as, Was the activity requested by the client?) were more objective than others (such as, Was the design appropriate to meet objectives?) and accordingly were less subject to observation errors. The indicators in the table average the responses across all tasks and are likely to average out the observation errors of responses on the individual knowledge activity.

cases where outcomes were likely to be sustained over time the knowledge activity conveyed international best practice and relevant examples, generated new evidence to inform policy making, and formulated actionable recommendations consistent with the findings. This was less often observed when knowledge activity results were partly likely or unlikely to be sustained. Similarly, when the results were likely to be sustained, knowledge services more often used local experts and discussed the capacity requirements and administrative feasibility of implementing the recommendations. Counterparts often said that use of local experts

TABLE 4.4 Sustainability of Knowledge Activity Outcomes in Relation to Knowledge Activity Characteristics Evaluated by IEG (in % of Knowledge Activity by Degree of Outcome Sustainability)

Indicators	Outcome of knowledge activity likely to be sustained		
	Yes	Partly	No
Activity conveyed international best practice and relevant examples	84.7	72	66.7
New evidence or data generated to inform decision making	78.6	64	50
Local expertise used by activity	60.2	40	27.8
Actionable recommendations consistent with findings were provided	74.5	74	55.6
Capacity requirements and administrative feasibility of recommendations discussed	50	46	22.2
Knowledge activity complemented by other World Bank activities	60.2	38	22.2
Activity contributed to developing or strengthening institutions	56.1	30	5.6
Activity contributed to strengthening analytical or policy formulation capacity of recipient	68.4	52	5.6

SOURCE: IEG knowledge activity reviews.

NOTE: Some questions on the tasks (such as, Was the activity requested by the client?) were more objective than others (such as, Was the design appropriate to meet objectives?) and accordingly were less subject to observation errors. The indicators in the table average the responses across all tasks and are likely to average out the observation errors of responses on the individual knowledge activity.

enhances the sustainability of knowledge activity results as it improves the applicability of the recommendations and helps build the local capacity needed for long-term impact. In addition, sustainability of outcomes was more often observed when knowledge services were complemented by other World Bank activities (lending, other ESW, or complementary TA). In the majority of cases where sustainability of outcomes was likely, knowledge services contributed to strengthening institutions or the analytical and policy formulation capacity of recipients. This was observed less often when outcomes were partly sustainable and was virtually not observed when sustainability was unlikely (box 4.3).

The South Africa Micro, Small, and Medium Enterprises (MSME) Study, conducted in 2004–06, was a follow-up to the Investment Climate Assessment. It reviewed the effectiveness of existing programs supporting MSME; provided new information through surveys; introduced new methodologies, such as the value chain approach; and provided actionable recommendations. While World Bank staff led the study, several local consultants prepared parts of the study, including the surveys and value-added analysis. The study was a major input to the government's MSME strategy, including an evaluation of the design of the MSME program. The Small Enterprise Development Agency was subsequently created to implement the MSME strategy, with the Department of Trade and Industry refocusing on the policy-making and strategy formulation functions. These changes strengthened the institutional framework for MSME development. At the same time, the study provided new methodologies (value chain analysis, evaluation of programs) that would be useful in policy formulation.

In a very different context, at the request of the authorities, the Bank provided support to the International Poverty Reduction Center in China (IPRCC) through three experience-sharing events from 2008 to 2010. These events aimed to facilitate the sharing of China's development experience with African policy makers and development practitioners. The activity led to a set of case studies and briefing notes that were used in the events and published by the client as training materials. Most presenters in these events were Chinese government officials, researchers from Chinese institutes, professors from Chinese universities, or IPRCC staff. The outputs were used to build the capacity of IPRCC and raise African participants' awareness of China's development experience. Another Bank TA activity, to the China-Development Assistance Committee (DAC) Study Group, worked with IPRCC on related topics. These two activities reinforced each other as the objective of the China-DAC Study Group was to help participants reach consensus on what is important in development assistance. IPRCC's analytical capacity improved through this training and research platform and this improvement is expected to be sustained. Both Bank activities contributed to building IPRCC's capacity to design and deliver training programs in the future. At the same time, knowledge gained by African officials is likely to benefit them in the long run. Although there were no clear indicators to measure the outcomes of the events, this activity, and its companion TA to the China-DAC Study Group, are among the few reviewed by the Independent evaluation Group (IEG) to have promoted South-South policy exchanges.

SOURCE: IEG knowledge activity reviews.

TABLE 4.5 Results Indicators of World Bank Group Knowledge Services

Indicators	Categories	Percentage			
		NA	No	Partly	Yes
Results indicators in CPS to measure the knowledge activity contribution to CPS development outcomes	World Bank Knowledge Activities	7.1	75.5	5.6	11.2
	IFC Advisory Services	3.1	37.5	9.4	50
Measureable results indicators included in knowledge activities	World Bank Knowledge Activities	11.7	64.8	10.2	12.8
	IFC Advisory Services	6.3	12.5	18.8	62.5

SOURCE: IEG knowledge activity reviews.
NOTE: NA = Not applicable. Some questions on the tasks (such as, Was the activity requested by the client?) were more objective than others (such as, Was the design appropriate to meet objectives?) and accordingly were less subject to observation errors. The indicators in the table average the responses across all tasks and are likely to average out the observation errors of responses on the individual knowledge activity.

Bank knowledge service results were not monitored and evaluated consistently for either the individual activity or the CPS.[4] IEG's review indicates that just 17 percent of knowledge services assessed in the focus countries had at least a partial results framework in the CPS making it possible to track the contribution of the activity to the broader development outcomes sought by the CPS (table 4.5). Similarly, only 23 percent of knowledge services included, at least partly, result indicators to track the achievement of the activity's outcomes. It is notable that, in contrast to Bank knowledge services, the majority of IFC Advisory Services reviewed by IEG were at least partly equipped with results indicators to trace achievement of outcomes. Although monitoring of capacity development outcomes and lessons learning were weak for Bank knowledge services, it appears that they were less so for knowledge services with outcomes likely to be achieved.

Synergy between World Bank and IFC Knowledge Services in Achieving Results

World Bank knowledge services and IFC Advisory Services[5] generally complement each other in contributing to results. Several factors influence the degree to which World Bank and IFC knowledge services have synergy. The main factor is the quality of the CPS results framework, in particular the articulation of CPS outcomes and the clarity of the linkage between the Bank

Group's programs, projects, and instruments with the CPS outcomes. Another factor is the existence of core ESW—such as ICAs and FSAPs—to underpin the strategy and help identify priorities for improving the investment climate and developing the financial sector. In a few cases, there were well-defined programs of joint World Bank and IFC knowledge activities. Nonetheless, the experience with coordination between the World Bank and IFC was mixed. There is scope for improving coordination between the World Bank and IFC, for example, by establishing more systematic mechanisms for inclusion of one institution in the other's review processes—especially at the concept and design stages.

In the case of South Africa, for example, all World Bank and IFC knowledge services covered by the review were intended to contribute to the private sector development component of the first pillar of the CPS, with the outcome defined as improved investment climate for labor-intensive informal and formal enterprises, focusing on MSME. Two ICAs and a major MSME ESW by the Bank were the core analytic work, followed by a series of World Bank and IFC knowledge activities that enhanced knowledge in various issues or themes identified in the core ESW. The distribution of follow-up work was based on the respective institutions' areas of expertise and experience, with the World Bank focusing on deeper analysis of exchange rate and labor regulations and IFC dealing with issues relating to administrative barriers or compliance costs faced by small businesses. In addition, IFC provided TA to three private sector institutions supporting small businesses, including two entrepreneurship programs, building on IFC experience with similar projects in the region. There are other thematic areas where the World Bank typically takes the lead, such as on tax issues, but IFC conducted two projects on MSME tax burden and compliance. To ensure synergy and coordination, IFC used experienced Bank staff to manage the projects. However, there seems to be a lack of clarity and poor coordination in the support to the Department of Trade and Industry where both World Bank and IFC provided TA—the World Bank, for example, had not received the report IFC prepared on competition policy.

In the South Africa financial sector, only one IFC project was reviewed, a three-year TA program to support MSME lending by improving credit information for smaller firms, an area where IFC has experience. Establishing credit bureaus and secured transactions regimes have become a major focus of the access to finance business line in Advisory Services. In addition, IFC is able to use its investments in the financial sector in South Africa to design a project that supports both the supply and demand side of credit information. In the process, it provides a demonstration of the benefits to encourage wider use of such information. The IFC Advisory Services in the financial sector support the CPS strategic component and the Bank's ESW on MSME. There is no overlap with other World Bank financial sector knowledge activity, which included an FSAP report and an ROSC on insolvency. Nonetheless, interviews with Bank staff indicated that coordination could be improved, especially given the increasing focus by the Bank on MSME financing.

In the case of the Russian Federation, the CPS aimed at strong progress in land registration and cadaster listings as a primary outcome of the pillar on sustaining rapid growth. Three of the five IFC activities reviewed focused on advancing administrative reforms in land or real estate transactions and complemented the World Bank Cadaster Project. In addition, two of the IFC real estate projects were managed by Bank staff, which reduced the risk of lack of coordination between the two institutions. Linked to the work on land is the IFC project to help develop the primary mortgage market, which would enable growth of secondary mortgage market and in the process deepen and broaden financial markets. As noted in the CPS Completion Report Review by IEG, the International Property Rights Index has improved slightly since the simplification of procedures and creation of the legal basis for a Unified Real Estate Cadaster. In addition, the World Bank's ICA provided an important basis for selecting Bank Group activities. World Bank knowledge activities reviewed by IEG were mainly in economic diversification, competition, and innovation, where the World Bank typically takes the lead, with IFC focusing on administrative barriers to investments, including an IFC project on lessons learned in reforming administrative barriers in the Russian Federation aimed to elicit discussion on effective strategies. In response to the government's demand for regional analysis in the investment climate work, the World Bank and IFC jointly delivered the Subnational Doing Business report, which was well received.

There was less coherence and coordination in the World Bank and IFC financial sector work in the Russian Federation in support of the CPS expected outcome of increased access to finance for entrepreneurs. The IFC work on securitization and insurance was not aligned with CPS emphasis on MSME financing, which was a major focus of IFC investments and supported by a World Bank study. The work on securitization did not produce the outcomes envisioned due to the financial crisis. In the case of insurance, the consolidation of the regulatory agencies left the ongoing IFC work uncertain on the way forward. One exception noted above is the work on mortgage development, which was linked to the land reforms and IFC investments in regional banks with mortgage lending portfolios. The World Bank AAA in the financial sector revolved around issues flagged in the FSAP Update, and was accompanied by work on crisis response, consumer protection, banking vulnerability assessment, payment system, and macro prudential tools. The Country Partnerships Strategy Completion report (CPSCR) Review by IEG concluded that the increased flow of financing to Russian entrepreneurs did not materialize as expected, though there were some improvements in capital market regulations.

In China, the World Bank ICA identified priorities to improve the investment climate in 120 cities. Five IFC projects complemented the ICA in two ways. First, an IFC project provided a monitoring tool for tracking the performance of various regions and cities, including the establishment of a baseline. Second, IFC provided TA—including to Sichuan province—to help identify and implement best practices in investment promotion. The work with Sichuan province, which has been experiencing significant increases in foreign direct investment flows over the past five years with IFC Advisory Services and investment support, would provide a demonstration of various investment promotion practices that could be replicated, with the help of central authorities, in other provinces. Nonetheless, there was only modest progress overall in simplifying cumbersome business regulations.[6] There was also an IFC project that supported the government in shaping its policies on corporate behavior, specifically in the areas of corporate governance, labor, and environmental and social practices. The Advisory Services contributed to the CPS outcome on adoption of best practice in corporate governance and social responsibility by publicly listed state-owned enterprises and large private corporations. Guidelines on corporate behavior have been issued for listed firms as well as state-owned enterprises under the State-Owned Assets Supervision and Administration Commission.

In the financial sector, World Bank knowledge services focused on the enabling environment for capital markets development while IFC Advisory Services projects were mainly addressing access to financial services, in line with the priorities in the CPS pillar on financing sustained and efficient growth. The World Bank produced the FSAP as well as knowledge products on financial stability, creditor rights, accounting and auditing, and capital markets. The World Bank also produced knowledge products on MSME financing—specifically, two papers for the People's Bank of China on microfinance and lending through intermediaries, to pave the way for a Bank loan to China Development Bank for MSME. IFC followed a programmatic approach to its work on MSME and complemented the Bank's knowledge and lending activities. The IFC project on SME Access to Finance was a focused nationwide survey to inform policy dialogue and raise stakeholder awareness. Three projects supported the development of a credit information system and secured transactions regime, starting with a review of the current institutional framework, followed by establishment of a pilot registry and finally by support for the operational phase of the system. As of the end of 2011, the credit reporting system covered more than 600 million individuals and another 18 million entities while the secured transactions system contributed to the 24 percent annual increase in loans using moveable assets during 2008–2010. Other IFC Advisory Services in the financial sector provided support for leasing and housing finance to improve access to financial services by introducing new instruments or lending products. Finally, the IFC Advisory Services leading to the enactment of the Personal Bankruptcy Law would help strengthen the legal framework affecting MSME lending. Interviews with staff indicate satisfactory coordination between IFC and World Bank Finance and Private Sector Development staff in Beijing.

Endnotes

[1] The share of investment lending operations for which IEG rated the development outcome moderately satisfactory or higher was 78 in FY06–08 and 70 percent in FY09–11 (projects exiting the active portfolio). The share of Development Policy Operations with a development outcome rating of moderately satisfactory or higher was 80 in FY06–08 and 83 percent in FY09–11. See Results and Performance of the World Bank Group 2012.

[2] Although in some cases the client did not take the Bank's advice, its knowledge was deepened. Indeed, in a number of cases clients requested knowledge services to inform an ongoing policy discussion.

[3] IEG is aware that in many instances brainstorming exercises are catered to a broad and diverse group of stakeholders. At the same time, the IEG team had a difficult time finding public minutes or notes of the results of a number of brainstorming sessions. IEG also recognizes that the Bank team working on Kazakhstan is developing formal results frameworks as part of the programmatic JERP structure and new country partnership strategies results framework.

[4] IEG is aware that since FY11 the Bank has adopted a three-pronged approach to improve results and measurement of knowledge services: (i) strengthening self-assessments; (ii) implementing client feedback instruments to elicit client assessment of the usefulness and relevance of our knowledge products; and (iii) ex-post review by external evaluators (IEG is analyzing how it could be part of this system). In this vein, the Operations Policy and Country Services department is encouraging operational staff to structure knowledge activities around clear monitoring indicators based on a theory of change.

[5] IEG understands that in recent years IFC introduced reforms to improve Advisory Services implementation: peer review and quality at entry, client agreement for all Advisory Services projects, detailed guidelines for client contributions, standardized results measurement frameworks, bi-yearly project supervision, annual client surveys, and project completion reports.

[6] See also IEG Review of CPSCR for China, 2012.

5 Conclusions

The Independent Evaluation Group's (IEG's) review of knowledge-based World Bank country programs has aimed to discern the factors contributing to knowledge service effectiveness. It finds that Bank Group knowledge activities have been strategically relevant in countries that do not rely much on its financial services. Clients value the Bank Group's ability to convey international best practice, act as a trusted knowledge broker, customize knowledge to the local context, and take a sensible approach to important multisectoral development issues. At the same time, the Bank Group's knowledge services in the focus countries, delivered through the Bank's knowledge services and the International Finance Corporation's (IFC's) Advisory Services, have a reasonably good record of achieving results with a fair likelihood of sustainability. As more emerging market economies are graduating from the World Bank's financial services and demanding programs with higher knowledge content, the Bank Group's challenge will be to build on this record to ensure that it remains a partner of choice for upper-middle-income countries.

To respond to this multifaceted challenge, the World Bank should organize internally to meet effectively the growing demand for knowledge-based partnerships, while offering a set of customized services through delivery mechanisms that help clients achieve sustainable results. This will involve well-informed choices in the way the Bank responds to multiple client demands, allocates limited own human and financial resources to knowledge-based partnerships, expands the frontier of engagement through appropriate use of Reimbursable

Advisory Services (RAS), and works with clients to track the achievement of results. Leveraging the knowledge acquired from these partnerships to make them available to lower-income countries would be an additional challenge given the vision the Bank Group aspires to fulfill as a Bank for the whole world.

This chapter summarizes the main lessons learned from the evaluation as they relate to three questions:

- How can the World Bank enhance its value proposition in knowledge-based partnerships?

- How can the World Bank delineate the scope and instruments of knowledge-based country programs?

- How can the Bank Group leverage its engagement in knowledge-based country programs?

How Can the World Bank Enhance Its Value Proposition in Knowledge-Based Partnerships?

Three preconditions seem particularly important for the World Bank to add more value for clients seeking a partnership with higher knowledge services content:

- Paying enough attention to the quality and relevance of knowledge services delivered to clients

- Emphasizing practical, "how to" advice in the form of options for action

- Understanding incentives and the political economy of reform and making good use of local expertise.

Attention to the quality and relevance of knowledge services is key for results— regardless of how those services are financed—and for shaping learning under the "science of delivery" that is central to the present Bank reform effort. Focus on quality is important for results in all Bank Group country partnerships, but it is paramount when results depend on knowledge services alone, with no support from financial resources or procurement of goods and services as in Bank lending operations. IEG's review revealed that the quality and relevance of Bank knowledge services appear to be correlated with the degree of achievement of expected outcomes, independently of whether knowledge services are funded through the Bank's own resources, cofinanced by the client, or entirely financed through RAS. Ensuring top-quality knowledge services requires effort on multiple fronts: relevance of design to respond to client concerns, customization of international best practice to local conditions and institutional or capacity constraints, generation of data to support evidence-based policy making, formulation of actionable recommendations that fit local administrative and political economy constraints, and timely product delivery to influence key decisions. The Bank's knowledge services will need to meet the highest standards on all of these fronts to help clients achieve development results.

Successful delivery of high-quality knowledge services that meets the above criteria requires highly experienced staff with global perspective and ability to deliver products on time. The quality and the technical competency of the team leader, who has to be an expert in the field, are of critical importance. In addition, the sustainability of RAS greatly depends on the quality products delivered to ensure continued commitment and interest of high-level officials. Therefore, the Bank needs to pay close attention to the expertise and availability of staff to ensure success of the knowledge-based program to generate "value for the government's money."

This was evident in Kuwait, where the level of the team's expertise proved crucial in the success of knowledge products. Where the Bank team was not well staffed there was reputation damage, as in the bank governance knowledge activity. This was also observed in South Africa, where strong and broad-based domestic consulting capacities are available and where some Bank work was underappreciated or perceived not to be of consistently high quality. The Bank should be cautious in engaging in RAS when the appropriate level of expertise cannot be mobilized in a timely fashion. It is important that the Bank be able to assemble a team that is available to work on the project for its duration, to minimize unnecessary delays due to staff rotation and work effectively with counterpart steering groups. The Bank needs to strengthen the quality assurance process for knowledge services—particularly through a reinvigoration of the internal peer review process—to ensure adequate technical quality of the products delivered to clients. The latter is essential for the Bank to maintain its unique position on the knowledge front through RAS.[1] The Bank should also be mindful of staff incentives, as participation in lending operations is typically seen as more rewarding for career development than participation in teams for the delivery of—even high profile—knowledge services. This may discourage the ablest and most experienced staff from participating in knowledge-based country programs and should be managed as part of staff career development.

Emphasizing the "how to" options, as opposed to the diagnostics and the "what to do" recommendations. Where knowledge services are delivered through RAS, clients expect focused and practical advice, with short documents that are operational rather than long documents heavy on diagnostics and generic advice, which are useful for the policy-setting agenda but less operational. Presenting options and scenarios of different actions, rather than what is often perceived by counterparts as "recipes," would enhance the credibility and impact of the Bank's work in upper-middle-income countries that demand programs with high knowledge content. Providing advice in the form of options for action would enhance client ability to own the final policy decisions, action plan, or strategy. In South Africa, for example, this was true for recommendations in sensitive areas such as labor, MSME policies, and land reform where follow-up discussion of options highlighted by knowledge services (such as ICAs) led to positive results. It is important that the options presented be based on best international practice and a deep understanding of countries' institutions. Only in this way can policy advice really become operational for counterparts.

More generally, emphasizing "how to" options may require a different approach in delivering knowledge services, one that involves much more time interacting with clients, access to experienced consultants, and consequently more resources. The experience with the distribution of projects between the World Bank and IFC, with the Bank focusing on policy and IFC on "how to" aspects, may be a workable model in the investment climate and financial sector work. In any case, the Bank may have to review the skills mix of knowledge service teams for meeting the expectations of clients that demand higher knowledge content. This would require a change in attitude by team leaders and consultants, who should be hands-on, practical, and policy-oriented. Teams may need to draw more on Development Economics Vice Presidency (DEC) resources to ensure high-quality research, and on high-level consultant expertise with practical experience to provide practical know-how. Where the Bank has a Country Office, its presence would have to be maintained—although probably resized to the level of client demand—to preserve the Bank's perceived comparative advantage in customizing international best practice to the local context. With very limited lending in most countries with knowledge-based programs, the sustainability of this business model would require a decisive move toward RAS.

Making an effort to understand the political economy of reform and maximize the use of local expertise. As in all countries around the world, of particular importance in countries with knowledge-based programs are the incentives of various stakeholders to carry out a reform program. Understanding these incentives could enhance the impact of the Bank's knowledge services by presenting options that address the concerns and constraints faced by different constituencies. This could, for example, have enhanced the effectiveness of Bank knowledge activity on regional development in Chile. In Kuwait, for some activities, although the Bank's recommendations were theoretically sound, they were considered not implementable in the current political economy of the country. In complex political environments, as is often the case in countries with knowledge-based World Bank programs, it is important for the Bank to identify and work with champions, provide them with ammunition to stay engaged in internal policy debates, and promote the reform agenda over time. This proved true in South Africa's private sector where successful projects were led by appropriate partners (small and medium enterprises [SME] banking and pro-poor tourism).

Bridging the gap between international good practices and local conditions could be facilitated by involving local experts more extensively. This would not only enhance the applicability of the recommendations but also build the local capacity to achieve longer-term impact. Recourse to local expertise would also help the Bank understand better the political economy of reform in specific areas where advice is requested. As revealed by IEG's review, use of local expertise was associated with a greater degree of achievement of knowledge service results in the focus countries as well as with a greater likelihood of their sustainability. In China, for example, the most effective knowledge products start with a request from the highest level of government. They also involve close collaboration with local experts from the beginning of the project, drawing on their expertise in data collection, analysis and formulation of recommendations, and follow-up. For IFC, programs that start with a project that reviews local context, including use of local working groups, have been successful in generating credibility and ownership of recommendations.

How Can the World Bank Delineate the Scope and Instruments of Knowledge-Based Country Programs?

The scope and content of a knowledge-based country program are typically circumscribed with the aim of matching as best as possible evolving government priorities over the country partnership strategy (CPS) cycle, according to the Bank's comparative advantage and expertise in responding to client demands. Beyond the guiding principles for the design of the CPS, some key considerations for deciding the appropriate scope of a knowledge-based country program and its instruments would include:

• Remaining engaged in specific areas over an appropriate period

• Remaining engaged in areas relevant to the client country's medium-term development agenda, beyond the scope of RAS

• Conducting broad consultation with stakeholders and dissemination of knowledge services

• Making the most of RAS on the basis of transparent but flexible criteria, to sustain a business model conducive to results

• Using implementation and results monitoring systems to track progress toward mutually agreed outcomes.

Staying engaged and responsive in the implementation phases of Advisory Services through appropriate instruments. IEG's review reveals that a main factor that often limits the impact of freestanding knowledge services is the lack of a follow-up instrument to support transformation of recommendations into actual policies and programs and support implementation. In the absence of lending, follow-up support should help clients translate recommendations from sound analysis into implementable actions that take into account local political and administrative constraints. Furthermore, in a complex political environment, such as found in most upper-middle-income countries, implementation needs time. To address these issues, IFC has used programmatic approaches that enable a program to be developed within a period commensurate with capacity. Ownership of the technical assistance (TA) program and the sense of urgency for reforms can also be lost with changes in political leadership and the economic environment. The need for "staying the course" was noted, for example, in Kuwait where, although clear results on knowledge services completed over the past five years are elusive, it is encouraging that gradual appropriation of these reforms has been built over time and some key legislation may be closer to being passed. This was facilitated when the Bank team stayed engaged over time to provide advice on best practice legislation—such as in procurement.

It is possible to design programmatic knowledge services that enable TA or economic and social work (ESW) to follow up on initial work. The work on innovation in the Russian Federation is a good example of such an approach. Initial work provided a set of innovation models to choose from, and follow-up knowledge activities would support design of the specific model chosen. Another example is the Doing Business report in the Russian Federation, where the country Doing Business analysis was followed up by similar regional analysis in response to feedback from stakeholders. Programmatic approaches would be pertinent in work on administrative barriers, economic diversification, small and medium enterprises (SME) development, and public finance management reforms. In Kazakhstan, the recent introduction of a programmatic Joint Economic Research Program (JERP) should help increase the strategic focus of knowledge services and provide room for more sustained sector policy dialogue. Moreover, the move toward a programmatic JERP should help attract and manage experienced Bank staff who will be engaged in a more consistent and challenging work program instead of smaller one-off activities.

In country partnerships based on knowledge services, engagement during implementation could be sought with a broader range of stakeholders, beyond the established government counterparts. Engaging systematically with civil society organizations (CSOs) could make the World Bank's knowledge services more effective. The objectives here could be to build CSO capacity, help disseminate the reform agenda, and maintain focus on key policy issues in the public domain. In Bulgaria, a good example of such partnerships was the Bank's association with the Open Society Institute—a local nongovernmental organization—on the judicial reform agenda, which was very helpful in carrying out relevant field work and disseminating results to the public. The Open Society Institute also has kept the topic in the public domain, which would have been difficult for the Bank to achieve on its own.

Remaining engaged in areas that are relevant to countries' medium-term development agendas. One pitfall of the "consultant firm model" that is often being used to respond to client demand through RAS is the possible lack of continuous engagement in some areas as a result of the drive to respond to multiple client demands. Another pitfall is the lack of coverage of thematic areas that may not rank sufficiently high on the short-term priorities of clients so as to be included in jointly financed RAS programs. These drawbacks may risk eroding the Bank's capacity to see the big picture and provide multisectoral development solutions—a strength of the Bank's knowledge services that is generally valued by clients. In Chile, for example, stakeholders noted that possible focus areas beyond the Joint Studies Program could include labor productivity, innovation policy, and climate change. The program in Chile is demand-driven, and the client has not requested Bank assistance in these areas, but the broader engagement may be necessary for the Bank to remain relevant in supporting Chile's development agenda. In Bulgaria, in parallel with helping the government implement the Europe 2020 strategy and absorb European Union (EU) funds, there is a role for the World Bank in continuing to raise awareness on issues beyond the RAS agreement, issues that are important for Bulgaria's medium-term development agenda, such as judicial sector reform. The Bank will need to think about the appropriate instruments to use (high-level brainstorming, conferences, ESW) and commit necessary resources, incremental to the resources allocated to programs jointly financed with clients. Using the instrument of an annual or bi-annual *Economic Monitoring Report* with focus on special topics may be an option to consider, in view of the successful record of these publications in Malaysia, Thailand, and China. For IFC, the CPS is an important guide to areas of engagement, making quality of the CPS and its results framework a critical factor in relevance and effectiveness of Advisory Services.

Conducting a broad consultative process and dissemination, acknowledging the public good function of Bank knowledge services, while paying attention to local circumstances. Based on IEG's review, client participation in the different stages of knowledge services appears to be closely associated with success in achieving expected knowledge service outcomes. Thus, the Bank should aim at bringing broader participation from various stakeholders into knowledge-based country programs—including by opening up discussions or establishing focus groups with local experts and CSOs. Broad dissemination of knowledge services that have the attributes of a "public knowledge good" (as defined in chapter 2 and Box 2.1), regardless of its mode of financing, would help strengthen the demand side for moving forward on the long-term reform agenda of country clients. Often, due to language and other difficulties, more time is needed for full outreach of the Bank's knowledge services. A single, short dissemination event may thus not have significant impact. Follow-up thematic discussion sessions may be appropriate and should not be neglected once the Bank's knowledge product has been formally delivered to the client.

Broad consultation and dissemination might be even more important in a complex political environment. In Kuwait, for example, presentations by the Bank of diagnostic work and reform recommendations or draft legislation (for example, on procurement and civil service) to government officials and parliament were helpful to build awareness of key issues. In Chile, engaging with a broader range of stakeholders through more informal channels, beyond the direct counterparts involved in the financing and vetting of knowledge services, such as high-level think tanks that exert an influence on the development agenda, would help enhance the impact and sustainability of the Bank's work. Consultations will need to extend beyond country clients when other development partners are involved. In Bulgaria, for example, as the implementation of the Europe 2020 agenda and the facilitation of the absorption of EU funds are main drivers of the Bank's new partnership strategy, it will be important to harmonize as much as possible the Bank's advice with that of EU institutions that frame Bulgaria's reform agenda. This will require very frequent exchanges with EU institutions at all levels of the Bank's country team.

Brainstorming sessions, while highly influential over policies, have the potential to become a confidential exercise where the Bank may be seen as a select advisor to very high-level officials, possibly with vested interests. Ways to avoid this could be to discuss with the authorities the possibility of opening sessions to interested stakeholders as needed, depending on the topic, and keeping full records, which could be disclosed at a specified time.

Although public demand for Bank analysis is generally high, dissemination is often hampered where knowledge services are provided through RAS. This is because RAS reports are often proprietary and subject to confidentiality. In several countries, such as Malaysia, the Bank has worked hard and with success to persuade the client to release these reports, but many studies remain inaccessible for most stakeholders for at least some time after their completion. The Bank and its clients could explore ways to make Bank studies more widely accessible to increase their impact. One option would be to recognize upfront the public good component inherent in several knowledge products. A portion of the knowledge service cost could be shared by the Bank on the condition that the resulting study would be released to the public shortly after completion. This approach has been considered by the World Bank in the recent review of Fee-Based Services.

However, it has to be acknowledged that, although broad consultations and strong dissemination efforts are key, the Bank should also be ready to "work behind the scenes" if local circumstances warrant. In South Africa, for example, in some sectors, the Bank should be willing to provide high-quality technical advice to the client on a confidential basis as needed, and be less preoccupied with dissemination. In such cases, the Bank would need to adapt its incentives and policies for recognition of staff work.

Although RAS do not seem to enable knowledge activities to get more traction on results, they should be systematically offered to clients with a view to ensuring the sustainability of the Bank's business model in knowledge-based country programs. The World Bank should continue offering RAS to countries that make limited use of its financing services but are seeking its knowledge to an extent that surpasses the Bank's financial capability to respond to this demand.[2] As the Bank bundles knowledge services with finance in all countries that use its lending services—with the cost of the knowledge services partly reflected in the pricing of the Bank's loans—offering knowledge services at no cost to countries that make limited use of the Bank's financing would risk diverting the Bank's resources away from clients most in need of assistance. Offering RAS is a win-win strategy for the Bank and its clients as it allows the Bank to expand the feasible set of services it provides to countries, while the continuous engagement with upper-middle-income countries on the knowledge front generates new knowledge that the Bank is in a unique position to intermediate to lower-income countries. However, IEG's review suggests that, although the relevance of RAS is strengthened by client demand and financial commitment, the results achieved do not appear significantly different from those of knowledge services funded by the Bank's own resources. Other fundamental factors—related to the relevance of design, quality, timeliness, client participation, and use of local expertise—are more closely associated with the achievement of results.

The Bank's policy regarding the pricing of RAS stipulates full cost recovery—including direct, indirect, and sustaining costs of the services (overhead).[3] Full cost recovery pricing does not preclude the Bank's participation in RAS financing. This occurred in practice, to varying degrees, in the evaluation's focus countries, for example, in Chile and Kazakhstan where the Bank cofinances joint studies programs. The 2012 review of Fee-Based Services conducted by the Bank provides an indicative framework for RAS pricing with the aim of increasing transparency and efficiency. According to this framework, the main criteria for pricing would be the recipient's income and ability to pay, the recipient's level of borrowing, public good externalities from disclosure, economies of scale related to the size of RAS, and the cost implications of risk management.

The new pricing framework is a step in the right direction. It could be complemented by clarifying the types of knowledge services that come close to pure public goods in nature (such as the *Economic Monitor* series in Malaysia and Thailand, or the Financial Sector Assessment Program [FSAP] and Report on the Observance of Standards and Codes [ROSC] reports), as opposed to those that serve specific needs of counterparts. The Bank should continue to fully fund studies that are pure public goods, while the cost of those studies that mostly benefit the client should be priced at full cost recovery. In countries with knowledge-based country programs, RAS could be offered to institutions that are in position to cover the full cost of the Bank's services. In Thailand, for example, this could be the case for self-funded organizations such as the Bank of Thailand (work on financial inclusion), the Credit Guarantee Corporation (work on SME master plan), and the Bank for Agriculture and Agricultural Cooperatives (work on risk management). Cost sharing of knowledge services that are not pure public goods could be determined based on the criteria selected by the Bank, with emphasis on the relevance of the activities for other countries and their disclosure by the recipient. The income criterion would also be important, especially to equalize access to the Bank's knowledge services among subnational clients with varying capacity to pay for the service—as in the case of the Russian Federation's regions. In addition, full cost recovery could include the cost of a client survey, to be conducted when the knowledge activity is completed with the aim of informing both the Bank and the client about the quality and relevance of the product, its use, and the results achieved or likely to be achieved. This would help the Bank to better track the quality of RAS supplied and learn more systematically about their use and the results achieved so as to better tailor them to client expectations over time.

Using implementation and results monitoring systems to track progress toward mutually agreed outcomes and mitigate the risk of fragmentation and loss of strategic focus intrinsic in RAS. RAS require flexibility to respond to changing client demand. But, on the downside, fragmentation of RAS programs often results from the commendable drive to accommodate multiple and unforeseen client needs. Flexibility would thus need to be balanced against the risk of fragmentation and an ensuing loss of strategic focus of the Bank's knowledge work through RAS programs. In the Russian Federation, for example, the considerable increase in knowledge services conducted under RAS since FY08 has reduced the predictability of the knowledge service program. Several of the originally planned knowledge activities in the FY07–11 CPS were dropped and new tasks were added. This could dilute the focus on the achievement of results sought by the country partnership. To mitigate these risks, first, it would be useful to elaborate a CPS in countries where knowledge-based country programs are being implemented without a CPS framework. A CPS with these countries does not have to be the outcome of a burdensome consultation process conducive to an elaborate document. The purpose of the CPS could be to provide guidance on the strategic priorities for World Bank Group engagement in the country to best leverage the expertise of the World Bank and IFC, avoid fragmentation of activities, and help plan efficiently the use of limited Bank resources. It would be, however, important to complement the CPS by a solid results framework. It is sometimes argued that sustained client demand for RAS is the best indication that a knowledge-based country program remains relevant and thus a CPS with a formal results framework could be redundant. However, this does not address the risk of fragmentation and diluted focus, nor the need for both the Bank and its clients to track results and learn from success and failure. Second, it would be important to use—and continuously refine—implementation and results monitoring systems that would track progress toward achieving the outcomes in the results framework of the CPS and more tightly link knowledge activities with CPS milestones and outcome indicators.

A RAS program could be enhanced if it contained a consultation mechanism between the Bank and the authorities, which would include the identification of results indicators at the inception of the tasks, and a follow-up review of the actions taken and results achieved. Problems related to absence of strong enough results frameworks are often exacerbated by the high level of client staff rotation within public services, which complicate the tracking of knowledge service recommendations and their implementation. Moving toward programmatic knowledge services should facilitate tracking of results over time, notably in areas with multiyear and interconnected Bank support. More generally, arrangements could be explored for sharpening the strategic relevance of rapidly evolving RAS programs. Options could include the establishment of funds cofinanced by the authorities and the Bank, with the possible participation of trust funds, with the aim of prioritizing programmatic knowledge services, knowledge services on important issues for the medium-term development agenda, or TA to lagging areas of the country.

How Can the Bank Group Leverage Its Engagement in Knowledge-Based Country Programs?

The synergy of World Bank knowledge activities and IFC Advisory Services projects could be strengthened. Developing robust results frameworks in country partnership strategies that articulate the CPS outcomes and their linkages with the Bank Group's programs and instruments is a key factor for enhancing the synergy between World Bank knowledge services and IFC Advisory Services in countries with World Bank knowledge-based partnerships. Synergy would also be enhanced by conducting core knowledge services for private and financial sector development—such as ICAs and FSAPs. Beyond the current practice of informal coordination between staff in country offices, there may be merit to establishing a formal mechanism of including each institution in the other's review processes.

Development of joint programs is another option to consider; this has been done in other countries. Joint projects—as in the Subnational Doing Business project and land registration projects in the Russian Federation—could also be used more often.

Improving the way the Bank learns from upper-middle-income countries and intermediates this knowledge to other countries. The Bank's engagement in countries with knowledge-based programs generates relevant knowledge for other, especially neighboring, countries. There is scope for improving the way the Bank intermediates knowledge generated through knowledge-based country programs. Exchanges could be enhanced within the Bank through communities of practice and outside the Bank through networks of practitioners. The recently launched Public Expenditure Management Network for Asia (PEMNA) is a good example of such a peer-based learning network of practitioners in public financial management. Portals on sector work in country office websites would also help share experiences. The role of the regional chief economists would also have to be enhanced, beyond the supervision of regional flagship reports, to linking up with regional think tanks and research institutions that can play a role in sharing the Bank's analytical work in knowledge-based partnerships across countries. Indeed in countries with a preponderance of knowledge services this role should not be assigned to a single position or unit, but chief economists are well positioned to take the lead and coordinate the linking work in knowledge-based partnerships. Easing the confidentiality of knowledge services conducted through RAS would also facilitate knowledge transfers. Steps in this direction suggested by a Bank review of fee-based services could somewhat alleviate this constraint.

More generally, technical capacity developed by upper-middle-income country clients could be leveraged more effectively in Bank knowledge work. Thailand, for example, has built capacity in banking, payments system, and financial markets. The Bank could leverage this capacity in other countries, rather than bringing in a large number of international consultants, which will also provide an opportunity for the Bank to partner with Thai institutions. The same applies to Malaysia's and Chile's experience, which is of great interest respectively to other Association of Southeast Asian Nations and Latin American countries. Through its regional hubs and staff working on neighboring countries, the Bank informally transmits, to some extent, to other countries the knowledge gained in countries such as Chile, Malaysia, and Thailand. However, more can be done as there is a sense that these South-South exchanges remain weak.

Table 5.1 summarizes the links between findings, lessons, and recommendations discussed in this report.

TABLE 5.1 Findings, Lessons, and Recommendations

IEG Findings	IEG Lessons	IEG Recommendations
Achievement of results from knowledge services was driven by their **relevance and technical quality,** including task designs that responded to client concerns; customization of international best practice to local conditions, including capacity constraints; generation of data to support policy making; formulation of actionable recommendations that fit local administrative and political economy constraints; and timely delivery of products to influence key decisions (par. 4.15).	Attention to the relevance and technical quality of knowledge services is essential for results—regardless of how knowledge services are financed—and for shaping learning under the "science of delivery" that is central to the present Bank reform effort.	Conduct broad consultation (with the client and other stakeholders) on the issues to be addressed; deploy highly experienced staff with global perspective and ability to deliver analytical and advisory activities (AAA) products on time; and adhere to the mandatory AAA quality assurance process. Encourage emerging knowledge hubs to follow approaches along these lines.
Most tasks referred to the **local policy context,** albeit in variable detail. Those that achieved results probed more deeply into local context (see pars. 3.9-3.13) and used local expertise more often than those that did not achieve results.	Understanding the political economy of reform and using local expertise can enhance the impact of the Bank's AAA. Local partners or hubs can also be critical in conveying relevant country context considerations.	Involve local experts, partners, and local knowledge hubs more extensively in AAA to help understand better the political economy of reform in the country where advice is sought, bridge the gap between international good practices and local conditions, enhance the applicability of the recommendations, and build the local capacity to achieve longer-term impact.
Tasks that achieved results provided **actionable recommendations** more often than those that did not achieve results.	Emphasizing the "how to" options, as opposed to the diagnostics and the "what to do" recommendations, will enhance a client's ability to own policy decisions, action plans, or strategies.	Give staff more time to interact with clients and local partners and knowledge hubs, including through adequate field presence; deploy available analytical expertise to ensure high-quality research underpinning recommendations and high-level consultant expertise able to provide practical know-how and enable customization of global practice.

continued on next page

TABLE 5.1 Findings, Lessons, and Recommendations *(continued)*

IEG Findings	IEG Lessons	IEG Recommendations
Use of **programmatic approaches** was important to achieve outcomes. There are examples of programmatic knowledge services that enabled technical assistance (TA) or economic and social work (ESW) to follow up on initial work (par. 5.14). In contrast, some projects launched in response to demand did not produce strong results, sometimes because these were one-off initiatives with poor sustainability prospects (par. 4.20).	Staying engaged and responsive in the implementation phases of Advisory Services through appropriate instruments can help clients translate recommendations from sound analysis into actions that fit local political and administrative constraints.	Design programmatic AAA in a number of thematic areas (for example, public financial management) that build on initial work to support implementation phases, including engagement of a broad range of stakeholders to help disseminate the reform agenda and maintain the focus on key policy issues in the public domain.
Complementing knowledge services with lending made results more likely to be sustained.	Close links between Bank ESW, nonlending TA, and projects may help sustain results.	Design country partnership strategies (CPSs) with closer links between knowledge activities and lending, including programmatic series deploying both instruments to support the paths from consideration of policy options to implementation of selected approaches.
Linking Bank with International Finance Corporation (IFC) activities also helped achieve results (see examples in pars. 4.23–4.29). But the experience with Bank-IFC coordination has been mixed, with quality of the CPS results framework and the existence of core ESW among the factors that influenced the degree to which World Bank and IFC knowledge services had synergy.	Stronger synergies between World Bank knowledge services and IFC Advisory Services projects can improve results.	Conduct core knowledge activities for private and financial sector development and develop joint Bank/IFC programs and projects within CPS results frameworks that articulate the outcomes and their linkages with the programs and instruments of both institutions. This would be complemented by formal mechanisms of including each institution in the other's review processes.

TABLE 5.1 Findings, Lessons, and Recommendations *(continued)*

IEG Findings	IEG Lessons	IEG Recommendations
The capacity to see the big picture and provide multisectoral development solutions has been a strength of the Bank's knowledge services, generally valued by clients. Delivery of knowledge services through a "consultant firm model," which reflects a drive to accommodate multiple and unforeseen needs, often results in fragmentation of Reimbursable Advisory Services (RAS) programs (for example, by dropping tasks linked to medium-term objectives to accommodate shorter-term needs) and may dilute the **focus on important medium-term issues.**	Remaining engaged in areas that are relevant to countries' medium-term development agenda may help the Bank maintain its capacity to see the big picture and provide multisectoral development solutions.	Prepare CPSs with countries where knowledge-based country programs are being implemented without a CPS (which does not have to follow a burdensome consultation process) to provide guidance on Bank Group engagement objectives and avoid fragmentation of knowledge activities away from evolving development priorities. Use instruments (such as high-level brainstorming, conferences, and ESW, including periodic Economic Monitoring Reports) and commit the necessary resources to identify, follow up, and sustain emphasis over time on issues that are important for medium-term development.
Client participation in the different stages of knowledge activities appears to be closely associated with success in achieving expected knowledge service outcomes.	Conducting a broad consultative process and dissemination, acknowledging the public good function of Bank knowledge services, while paying attention to local circumstances, may improve results.	Broaden the participation of various stakeholders and local knowledge hubs into knowledge-based country programs (for example, by opening up discussions or focus groups with local experts and CSOs) and make Bank studies more widely accessible (for example, by recognizing upfront the public good component in knowledge products and sharing a portion of the knowledge service cost with the client on the condition of its disclosure).

continued on next page

TABLE 5.1 Findings, Lessons, and Recommendations *(continued)*

IEG Findings	IEG Lessons	IEG Recommendations
Bank knowledge activities were **not monitored and evaluated consistently in the sample of countries** (par. 4.22). Where it was, better knowledge service results were more likely to be achieved, probably reflecting a link between monitoring and evaluation (M&E), knowledge service quality, and impact.	Implementation and results monitoring systems are needed to track progress toward mutually agreed outcomes and mitigate the risk of fragmentation and loss of strategic focus intrinsic in RAS.	Use—and continuously refine—implementation and results monitoring systems that would track progress toward achieving the outcomes in the results framework of the CPS and that more tightly link knowledge activities with CPS milestones and outcome indicators. A "circle of continuous quality improvement" of M&E is critical for shaping the science of delivery that the Bank is presently intent upon and to help improve M&E at the country level.
There were ample opportunities for **learning from development experiences** in the focus countries (for example, on development trajectory from low-income to upper-middle-income economy in Malaysia or the extensive work the Bank has done in China on regional approaches to investment promotion).	There is scope to improve the way the Bank learns from upper-middle-income countries and intermediates this knowledge to other countries.	Enhance exchanges of knowledge within the Bank through communities of practice and outside the Bank through networks of practitioners or knowledge hubs; enhance the links of the Bank's regional chief economists with regional institutions that can play a role in sharing the Bank's analytical work; ease the confidentiality of knowledge activities conducted through RAS; and leverage the technical capacity developed by upper-middle-income clients to other countries. This will also provide opportunities for the Bank to strengthen partnerships with local institutions in countries with knowledge-based programs.

TABLE 5.1 Findings, Lessons, and Recommendations (continued)

IEG Findings	IEG Lessons	IEG Recommendations
Although the relevance of RAS is strengthened by client demand and financial commitment, the achieved results do not appear significantly different from those of knowledge services funded by the Bank's own resources. Other fundamental factors—related to the relevance of design, quality, timeliness, client participation, and use of local expertise—are more closely associated with the achievement of results.	Although RAS do not seem to enable knowledge activities to get more traction on results, they help expand the feasible set of services it provides to countries, ensure the sustainability of the Bank's business model in knowledge-based country programs, and generate new knowledge that the Bank can then intermediate to lower-income countries.	Move decisively toward RAS in knowledge-based programs to sustain this business line, while clarifying the types of knowledge products that come close to "public knowledge goods" (Bank-funded reports targeted to a broad audience to disseminate analyses of developments or particular sectors or issues), as opposed to those that serve specific needs of counterparts. RAS could be offered to institutions that can cover the full cost of the Bank's services, with cost-sharing of knowledge products that are not public knowledge goods in recognition of the relevance of the activities for other countries. In those products where there is cost-sharing, there should be wider disclosure or dissemination by the recipient for equalization of access to the Bank's knowledge services. Full cost recovery could include the cost of a client survey, with the aim of informing both the Bank and the client about the relevance, quality, use, and results achieved or likely to be achieved.

Endnotes

[1] IEG understands that the Bank is in the process of improving the internal peer review process to ensure good technical quality of knowledge services.

[2] IEG understands that the Bank is applying the three-pronged monitoring approach (see endnote 24) to RAS, and developing more detailed guidance for staff application of operational policies to the RAS program.

[3] See Operational Memorandum on "The Provision of Fee-Based Services," updated in 2008 and proposed update in October 2012. Indirect and overhead costs have been approximated in the past by a factor of 50 percent of direct costs, unless actual estimates are available.

Bibliography

China Securities Regulatory Commission. 2008. *China Capital Markets Development Report.* Almanac of China's Finance and Banking Editorial Board. Beijing: China Securities Regulatory Commission.

Clarke, George R.G., James Habyarimana, Michael Ingram, David Kaplan, and Vijaya Ramachandran. 2007. *South Africa: An Assessment of the Investment Climate.* Washington, DC: World Bank.

Hausmann, Ricardo, Akash Deep; Rafael Di Tella; Jeffrey Frankel, Robert Lawrence; Dani Rodrik; and Andrés Velasco. 2011. "Growth and Competitiveness in Kazakhstan: Issues and Priorities in the Areas of Macroeconomic, Industrial, Trade and Institutional Development Policies." Working Papers, Center for International Development, Harvard University, Cambridge, Mass.

Hawkins, Loraine, Jaruayporn Srisasalux, and Sutayut Osornprasop. 2009. *Devolution of Health Centers and Hospital Autonomy in Thailand: A Rapid Assessment.* Washington, DC: World Bank.

Hinz, Richard P., Asta Zviniene, and Anna-Marie Vilamovska. 2005. *The New Pensions in Kazakhstan: Challenges in Making the Transition.* Social Protection Discussion Paper No. 0537. Washington, DC: World Bank.

IEG (Independent Evaluation Group). 2007. *Development Results in Middle-Income Countries: An Evaluation of the World Bank's Support.* Washington, DC: World Bank.

———. 2008. *Using Knowledge to Improve Development Effectiveness: An Evaluation of World Bank Economic and Sector Work and Technical Assistance, 2000–2006.* Washington, DC: World Bank.

———. 2009. *Independent Evaluation of IFC's Development Results: Knowledge for Private Sector Development.* Washington, DC: World Bank.

———. 2010. *World Bank economic reports on growth diagnostics in four African countries: Ghana, Mauritius, Nigeria, and Uganda.* Performance Assessment Review. Washington, DC: World Bank.

———. 2011. *Performance Assessment Review of Investment Climate Assessments in Five Transforming Economies: Bangladesh, Egypt, Guatemala, Kenya, and Vietnam.* Washington, DC: World Bank.

———. 2011. *World Bank Support for Revenue Policy Reform in Eastern Europe and Central Asia: With Performance Assessment Reports of ESW in Georgia, Kazakhstan and Kyrgyz Republic.* Washington, DC: World Bank.

———. 2012. *Results and Performance of the World Bank Group 2012.* Washington, DC: World Bank.

IFC (International Finance Corporation). 2012. *IFC Secured Transactions Advisory Project in China.* Washington, DC: World Bank

IMF (International Monetary Fund). 2008. "Thailand: Financial System Stability Assessment." IMF Country Report No. 09/147. Washington, DC: IMF.

———. 2010. "Russian Federation: Financial Sector Stability Assessment Update." IMF Country Report No. 10/96. Washington, DC: IMF.

———. 2010. "Kuwait: Financial System Stability Assessment—Update." IMF Country Report No. 10/239. Washington, DC: IMF.

———. 2011. "Chile: Financial System Stability Assessment." IMF Country Report No. 11/261. Washington, DC: IMF.

———. 2011. "China: Financial System Stability Assessment." IMF Country Report No. 11/321. Washington, DC: IMF.

Organisation for Economic Co-operation and Development (OECD). *Reviews of National Policies for Education: Higher Education in Kazakhsta.* OECD: Paris.

Revenga, Ana, Mead Over, Emiko Masaki, Wiwat Peerapatanapokin, Julian Gold, Viroj Tangcharoensathien, and Sombat Thanprasertsuk. 2006. *The Economics of Effective AIDS Treatment: Evaluating Policy Options for Thailand.* Washington, DC: World Bank.

World Bank. 2003. *Thailand—Country Assistance Strategy for FY03–FY05.* Washington, DC: World Bank.

———. 2005. "The Road to Successful EU Integration.The Policy Agenda Poverty Reduction and Economic Management Unit. Europe and Central Asia Region. Country Economic Memorandum." Washington, DC: World Bank.

———. 2006. "Thailand Investment Climate, Firm Competitiveness and Growth." Washington, DC: World Bank.

———. 2006. *Country Partnership Strategy for the Russian Federation for Period FY2007–FY2009.* Report No. 37901-RU. Washington, DC: World Bank.

———. 2006. *Russian Federation—Institutional Reform in Russia: Moving from Design to Implementation in a Multi-Level Governance Context.* Washington, DC: World Bank.

———. 2007. *Bulgaria—Accelerating Bulgaria's Convergence: The Challenge of Raising Productivity.* 2 vols. Washington, DC: World Bank.

———. 2007. *Chile—Country Partnership Strategy for the Period 2007–2010.* Washington, DC: World Bank.

———. 2007. *Republic of Kazakhstan—Report on the Observance of Standards and Codes (ROSC): Accounting and Auditing.* Washington, DC: World Bank.

———. 2007. "South Africa Enhancing the Effectiveness of Government in Promoting Micro, Small and Medium Enterprise." Washington, DC: World Bank.

———. 2007. *South Africa—Country Partnership Strategy for the Period 2008–2012.* Washington, DC: World Bank.

———. 2007. *An Assessment of the Investment Climate in South Africa.* Washington, DC: World Bank.

———. 2008. "Chile: Estudio de Evaluación en Profundidad del Programa de Mejoramiento de la Gestión (PMG)." Vol. 1. Washington, DC: World Bank.

———. 2008. *Bulgaria -- Resourcing the Judiciary for Performance and Accountability: A Judicial*

Public Expenditure and Institutional Review. Washington, DC: World Bank.

———. 2008. *Bulgaria—Country Partnership Strategy for the Period 2007–2009.* Washington, DC: World Bank.

———. 2008. *Thailand—Investment Climate Assessment Update.* Washington, DC: World Bank.

———. 2009. "Financial Sector Assessment Republic of Kazakhstan." Washington, DC: World Bank.

———. 2009. "Institutional Framework for Early Childhood Development in Chile." Policy Note. Report No. 71693. Washington, DC: World Bank.

———. 2009. *Bulgaria Social Assistance Programs: Cost, Coverage, Targeting and Poverty Impact.* Washington, DC: World Bank.

———. 2009. *Bulgaria: Living Conditions before and after EU Accession.* Human Development Sector Unit and Ministry of Labor and Social Policy. Washington, DC: World Bank.

———. 2009. *Bulgaria—Railways Policy Note.* Washington, DC: World Bank.

———. 2009. *Case Study on the Management of Chile's Social Security Reform: A Client-Focused, Public-Private System with the Support of IT Solutions.* Washington, DC: World Bank.

———. 2009. *China—Report on the Observance of Standards and Codes (ROSC)—Accounting and Auditing.* Washington, DC: World Bank.

———. 2009. *Malaysia Productivity and Investment Climate Assessment Update.* Washington, DC: World Bank.

———. 2009. *Russian Federation Regional Development and Growth Agglomerations—The Longer Term Challenges of Economic Transition in the Russian Federation—A Country Economic Memorandum for Russia.* Washington, DC: World Bank.

———. 2010. "Kuwait Public Expenditure and Financial Accountability Public Financial Management Performance Assessment Report." Washington, DC: World Bank.

———. 2011. "The State of World Bank Knowledge Services: Knowledge for Development 2011." Washington, DC: World Bank.

———. 2011. "La agenda de la descentralización en Chile: Propuestas de corto y mediano plazo para mejorar la gestión, fortalecer la rendición de cuentas y asegurar el control de resultados en el nivel municipal." Washington, DC: World Bank.

———. 2011. *Bulgaria—Country Partnership Strategy for 2011–2013.* Washington, DC: World Bank.

———. 2011. *Chile—Country Partnership Strategy for the Period FY11–FY16.* Washington, DC: World Bank.

———. 2011. *Chile's State-Guaranteed Student Loan Program: Analysis and Evaluation. (CAE).* Washington, DC: World Bank.

———. 2011. *Improving the Business Environment for Growth and Job Creation in South Africa: The Second Investment Climate Assessment.* Washington, DC: World Bank.

———. 2011. *Malaysia: Moving up the Value Chain—A Study of Malaysia's Solar and Medical Device Industries.* Washington, DC: World Bank.

———. 2011. *Public Sector Reforms and Human Resources for Health in Thailand: An Exploration of Impacts, Issues and Options for Moving Forward.* Washington, DC: World Bank.

———. 2011. *Reducing Inequality for Shared Growth in China: Strategy and Policy Options for Guangdong Province.* Washington, DC: World Bank.

———. 2011. *Russian Federation—Country Partnership Strategy for the Period 2012–2016.* Washington, DC: World Bank.

———. 2011. *Improving the Business Environment for Growth and Job Creation in South Africa: the Second Investment Climate Assessment.* Washington, DC: World Bank.

———. 2011. *Harm Reduction Policies and Interventions for Injection Drug Users in Thailand.* Washington, DC: World Bank.

———. 2012. *Bulgaria—Public Expenditures for Growth and Competitiveness.* Washington, DC.

———. 2012. *China 2030: Building a Modern, Harmonious, and Creative High-Income Society.* Washington, DC: World Bank.

———. 2012. *Integrated Air Pollution Management in China: Developing Particulate Matter Control.* Washington, DC: World Bank.

———. 2012. *Kazakhstan—Country Partnership Strategy for the Period FY12–FY17.* Washington, DC: World Bank.

———. 2012. *Leading with Ideas: Skills for Growth and Equity in Thailand.* Washington, DC: World Bank.

———. 2012. *Malaysia: Report on the Observance of Standards and Codes (ROSC), Corporate Governance Country Assessment.* Washington, DC: World Bank.

———. 2012. *The Basel III Financial Architecture and Emerging Regulatory Developments in Macro Prudential Tools.* Washington, DC: World Bank.

———. 2012. *The Provision of Reimbursable Advisory Services. Operational Memorandum.* Washington, DC: World Bank.

World Bank and Department of Land Affairs (South Africa). 2007. "Accelerating Sustainable, Efficient and Equitable Land Reform: Case Study of the Qedusizi/Besters Cluster Project." Africa Region Working Paper Series No. 109. Washington, DC: World Bank.

World Bank and Foreign Investment Advisory Service (South Africa). 2006. Sector Study of the Effective Tax Burden: South Africa. Washington, DC: World Bank.

World Bank and International Finance Corporation. 2012. "Kazakhstan Enterprise Survey." Washington, DC: World Bank.

World Bank and Ministry of Public Health (Thailand). 2010. Revitalising HIV prevention in Thailand: a critical assessment. Final report. Washington, DC: World Bank.

World Bank and Office of the National Economic and Social Development Board (Thailand). 2008. "Towards a Knowledge Economy in Thailand." Washington, DC: World Bank.

Yusuf, Shahid, and Kaoru Nabeshima. 2009. *Tiger Economies Under Threat: A Comparative Analysis of Malaysia's Industrial Prospects and Policy Options.* Washington, DC: World Bank.

Yusuf, Shahid. 2010. *People's Republic of China: China PSD Program.* Washington, DC: World Bank.

Zhang, Chunlin, Douglas Zhihua Zeng, William Peter Mako, and James Seward. 2008. *Promoting Enterprise-Led Innovation in China.* Washington, DC: World Bank.

www.ingramcontent.com/pod-product-compliance
Lightning Source LLC
Chambersburg PA
CBHW082358270326
41935CB00013B/1673